Discipline

Discipline

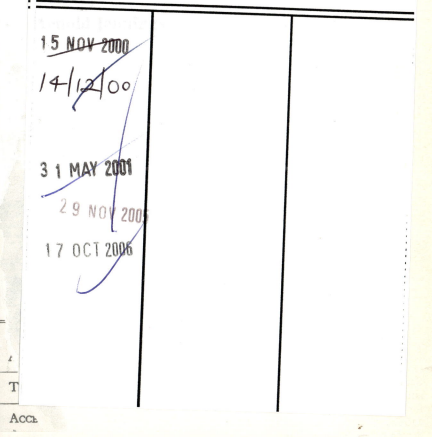
Ward Lock Educational

ISBN 0 7062 3814 1

First published 1979

Set in 10 on 11 point Monotype Plantin
and printed by Latimer Trend & Company Ltd, Plymouth
for Ward Lock Educational
116 Baker Street, London W1M 2BB
A member of the Pentos Group
Made in Great Britain

Contents

Introduction

Discipline in schools today is a favourite topic of journalists, TV commentators, politicians, industrialists and many others. It seemed it might contribute to the general debate to invite a number of people all of whom are involved, all but one professionally involved, every day with this to give their views on it and their account of it. They include some who are professionally in a position to make valid generalizations because they see the inside of a large number and a wide range of schools and to make judgments on what they see.

The twelve people invited to contribute include eight who are teachers in school and four who are not. The eight teachers include two from primary schools, one from a middle school and five from secondary schools; one of these schools is in inner London, two on the outskirts of London, one in a rural area and four in industrial cities in the north of England. Of the four who are not teachers, three have worked as teachers and are professionally engaged in education. Most of the contributors are parents of school children; one is a parent of school children who is not and never has been a teacher or professionally engaged in education. Four of the contributors are not in school and can speak without any bias that might be thought to imply; one is not engaged in education and therefore can speak without any bias at all. Elizabeth Wallis, whom I asked to contribute a parent's view, wrote to me, 'It is very difficult to assess the right note to strike when you know that yours will be the only chapter to represent parents in such a book. But then perhaps your book will also represent quite accurately the status accorded to parents in the British education system. I expect it [her chapter] will stick out like a sore thumb.'

Each contributor was asked to write on the subject of discipline in schools today, but to write on it from his/her own personal point of view, from his/her own perspective, drawing on his/her background and experience and often quoting actual examples and case histories. No editorial unity of views or outlook has been imposed or of topics or treatment within the single common heading. Certain themes do recur and emerge as common to a number of the writers. One thing that comes across is the caring, thoughtful, detailed, professional concern for the welfare, upbringing and training of the children in a school's care. Some may say these writers are not typical. I would think that in this they are.

I

They may in good faith be going on the wrong lines, at least on what some would consider to be the wrong lines. *Quot homines, tot sententiae*; there is no shortage of different opinions. There is no easy answer either and no one with an answer can be sure that he is right, or would ever say his was the only answer, only that it is his answer, and that he has tried it and found that it works.

No reference will be found in this book to 'blackboard jungles', although each writer writes fairly of his/her own experience, in many cases from long experience, nor any great speculation about whether standards of discipline are much lower than in the past. Several contributors say that discipline is harder to maintain today, which is something different, and offer reasons why this may have come about. One chapter begins with a typical complaint that the young today lack the discipline and the respect for authority that they used to have in the good old days and then reveals that the complaint is made by Plato, put into the mouth of Socrates, writing in the fourth century B.C. Sir Edward Britton used to quote a case that occurred in one of the public schools at the beginning of the nineteenth century where some boys roasted another boy to death in front of a fire; the parents, when they came to see the headmaster, agreed that this could be regarded as a typical boys' prank. The hero of *Westward Ho!* begins his adventures by 'breaking the head' of his teacher with his slate, and he (the hero) is treated in a wholly sympathetic way by the author, in this as in his later adventures.

Whether discipline now is better or worse – or just different – from what it was at any particular other time is perhaps not a very profitable question, but rather whether it is good enough, whether the general level is acceptable. Only those with inside knowledge of a wide range of schools today are in a position to pronounce on this. Neither of the contributions from school inspectors (LEA) would suggest that there is any general cause for alarm. The survey of the nation's primary schools by HMI just published also raises no such suggestion. The survey of secondary schools recently carried out by HMI is not yet published as I write, though it may well be by the time this book appears. I shall wait with interest – and quiet confidence – to see if it suggests anything seriously amiss in this regard in the nation's secondary schools, viewed as a whole. No one is perfect, no teacher, no head, no school; human fallibility and frailty guarantee plenty of shortcomings, but there does not appear to be reliable evidence that would indicate a general alarming state of indiscipline in the schools today.

Schools reflect society. In turn, society uses its schools to prepare its children for the kind of society it wishes to perpetuate, namely the *status quo*. But society changes constantly. Ours today is an increasingly violent society; the ready resort to violence is seen by our children daily in the newspapers and on TV, not only in the crime reports but in the political reports, as well as on the football grounds, on the terraces and on the field. It is a period of rapid change. It is one of those recurring times of a revolt against authority, often encouraged on very high-minded, if not very practical, grounds. It is a period of pluralism, in which there are few canons that command universal or even general acceptance, in which on major matters of how to live different people have sharply conflicting opinions. This directly affects our schools. It affects the climate in which they operate, it affects the attitudes the children bring with them to the schools, it affects the attitude of their parents and the public towards what the schools do.

I hope those who are interested in formulating their own views on these matters, on discipline in our schools today, will find these essays helpful. I hope this might apply to parents of school children and to teachers too.

November 1978   *Arnold Jennings*

1 The teacher-training aspect

John Anderson
Principal, The College of St Mark and St John, Plymouth

'Our youth now loves luxury. They have bad manners and contempt for authority. They show disrespect for their elders and love idle chatter instead of exercise.'
(Socrates: 470–399 B.C.)
'What can you get with CSE in Art and Rural Studies?'
(Barry Hines 1976)

Since the introduction of compulsory education we have come to expect schools to carry out five basic functions:

1 to organize, guide and support effective learning
2 to socialize the young in the prevailing values and behavioural norms in our society
3 to identify ability and to provide the basis for selection for future employment
4 to provide a sanctuary for all children during recognized working hours
5 to act as a reference point for child welfare including health checks and remedial treatment for handicaps.

As in any other institution good discipline is an essential to success. However, if one considers the various functions of the school it is clear that forms of control which teachers use have a qualitative effect upon the results achieved.

Learning is a complex process, but the starting point is motivation. Whilst teachers have to establish an ordered environment for learning they also have to secure the enthusiasm of their pupils. The techniques used to achieve control in a group situation clearly affect the individual's willingness to participate. The ideal is to encourage all concerned. In practice, for a variety of reasons, particularly the natural wilfulness of healthy, energetic children, encouragement needs to be set within a context of firmness with the judicious use of sanctions. But balance is critical since, whilst children will accept that punishment is occasionally needed to secure order, once it becomes over-used it becomes self-defeating, in that pupils lose respect for the school, its values and the enjoyment of learning.

5

In most cultures growing up involves tussles between young and old. Today much of the 'generation game' is played out in the school system, and it is a factor of which pupils and teachers are permanently aware. It is an important part of the process of self-discovery that at some time children should seek to 'play up', to test the authority of their elders or react with impatience towards adult control. Most of the evidence however has suggested that in general pupils expect and respect firmness, even strictness, from the teachers, providing that reasons are made clear and decisions are seen to be fair.

Put very simply, discipline is about living happily in school and is as much about ends as means. Thus a teacher sees his methods of control as an integral part of his craft; dependent not just upon scientific understanding of the job in hand, but personal sensitivity and commitment to his pupils as well.

In general teachers use techniques that engender cooperation, reasoned respect for authority and self-discipline: the virtues of the good citizen and the good worker. Indeed, many schools were founded with just this intention, for concern about discipline has a long history. Today, however, the social and political implications of what teachers are doing are becoming more obvious. Thus the forms of discipline used attract increasing attention. Pressure groups representing interests of all kinds: parents, employers, Trade Unions, children's rights, the pupils themselves, now speak out. The major political parties and the media are alert to this and naturally tend to exploit it. The noise of battle now sounds on nearly every educational issue, suggesting that there is a much more significant 'struggle for the school' going on outside the classrooms than in them. Such influences are likely to become stronger, although the speed of change is deceptive and our forecasting crude. One aspect of current concerns is that we may well be arguing about yesterday's problems: for instance, training a workforce for current requirements may have less real significance than preparing for the impact of microprocessing techniques.

But there is now evidence of new and urgent problems of disturbance, truancy and apathy in some schools. At present the dimensions are not clear, but it appears that only a minority of schools are seriously affected. These are located largely in cramped inner-city areas, and ill-provided housing estates, where wages are likely to be low and unemployment high. In the inner city, tensions may be heightened as a result of different ethnic and cultural groups living in close proximity, whilst on many vast housing estates life is so anonymous that communal disapproval is largely ineffective. This indicates that the situation in these schools arises from complex social and economic causes, and raises the question whether schools can and should be used to counteract social and economic deprivation.

This issue is apparent in the dilemma now facing the comprehensive school. It is designed to care for each pupil, encouraging him to find his

6

talents and interests and to develop them as a person in his own right and as a citizen ready to participate in a better future for all. Yet, at the same time, it tests pupils on the basis of their academic performance and sorts them into career pathways ranging from the O and A level classes which offer the best employment prospects, to the non-examination and remedial classes leading to dead-end jobs, poor wages and, with increasing probability, unemployment. This apparent incompatibility of function puts the relationship between teacher and pupil at the centre of one of modern democracy's most difficult dilemmas: how to establish a just and equal society to everyone's satisfaction while at the same time developing the talent which an advanced technological nation in a competitive world needs.

Almost every parent and pupil is aware of the competitive aspect in schooling, and for many this involves an increasing sense of failure and rejection so that by the time a child reaches early adolescence, both parent and pupil feel that the effort of sitting in a classroom and concentrating upon spelling or punctuation is not only counter to immediate inclinations but is also pointless in the long term as well. Sadly this has a perverse rationality about it, for without the right credentials society does treat school leavers as failures and offers them little in return for any marginal improvements they may make.

Our economic system shows marked diminishing returns to effort in the non-examination streams of the secondary school and here the growing prospect of unemployment is critical. For most young people the process of leaving school and entering wage-earning employment has great significance. It is, in effect, initiation into adulthood. The failures in academic work and the inconvenience of being treated as a child are left behind and independence and the respect of one's fellows seem assured.

Pressures upon the economy are altering this and with the growing tendency to hold schools to account over discipline, the relationship between school and the world of work or that of unemployment takes on a new significance. Many complaints come from employers apparently unable to find as direct entrants the conscientious workforce they want. Yet whilst they may vent their frustration about the quality of new workers, these same employers have fewer and fewer jobs on offer. Consequently, good behaviour in school is less a guarantee of a job than in earlier decades and so a critical sanction within the school system is being undermined.

The educational philosophy on which teachers have been nurtured has emphasized the neutrality of educational institutions, the importance of avoiding vested interests and the teacher's freedom to decide upon the curriculum and the methods of handling relationships with pupils. At the same time, this philosophy has increasingly emphasized individual rights and individual worth. To accommodate this and to move with the democratic spirit, most teachers try to encourage participation and approaches to order which stand up to reason. In doing so, however, they have to become much more personally involved with their pupils, depending not only upon carefully practised skills but a genuine concern for pupils as people and the emotional maturity to handle the more complex relationships this involves.

Ill-informed criticism of the lack of discipline in schools strikes at a very sensitive spot, especially when teachers have to draw upon personal resources and emotional energy to counteract over-crowded and under-resourced classrooms, whilst their loudest critics support cuts in public expenditure and keep much needed colleagues idle.

Union spokesmen for the teaching profession give conflicting responses; one tendency is to minimize worries and invoke professional integrity, another emphasizes the violence teachers now face and argues that teachers should only be concerned with those who want to learn. This not only reflects the division in the profession which weakens any corporate voice teachers might have, but also shows how teachers' unions in the present competitive atmosphere become pressure groups themselves, using opportunistic and short-term arguments. Unfortunately, this tends to confuse the debate further. Although there are marked differences between teachers, few seek to abdicate from public expectations of the school system and there are a growing number of attempts to enquire and explore into the question of discipline and its implications as clearly and honestly as possible. At one level teachers have become much more conscious about the techniques of classroom management and increasingly there are attempts to identify and develop skill and understanding with particular reference to the preparation and suitability of lessons, and firmness and sensitivity in making relationships. At an institutional level, a similar process of re-thinking has begun, with new approaches to corporate responsibility amongst teachers, counselling and pupil welfare services, attempts to isolate 'difficult' pupils and provide special attention in sanctuary units or remedial centres, new external support through truancy/intermediate treatment centres and attempts to give a new purpose to schools through links with industry and community service.

It is becoming increasingly obvious, however, that efforts to improve the skills and structure of internal management can only go so far. Schools cannot be isolated from the influences around them, nor should they be; for education, particularly where values are concerned, is a process involving a complex pattern of interacting institutions, of which the school is only one part: the family, the peer group, the neighbourhood and the media are others. In theory, schools should be able to communicate and, where possible, cooperate with other institutions, particularly the family. In practice this is much more difficult than it seems. Within present institutional structures there are few established links, indeed the tendency in the past has been to separate. Time and expertise to make links are not easily found and, as yet, good home–school relationships depend largely upon the willingness of teachers to give their own time.

8

Parents who have confidence are often prepared to cooperate, but where the home is suspicious, great demands are placed upon the teacher's time and sensitivity. Naturally enough teachers respond in very different ways, for the balance between friendliness and professional dignity is difficult to strike. Yet, for those who choose to emphasize explanation and cooperation, there is a marked irony in the way in which the society around them increasingly reflects conflict; the tendency to challenge officialdom and question management and to argue about who gets what. Indeed, our materialism and pluralism are usually reflected in contentious form by the media every day, with devastating effect upon family life and youth culture.

Many people assume that somehow the school is the control valve in the institutional circuit and can be used to shut off the more disruptive features of change. In a democratic society schools cannot do this. Of course they can try to arrange for a sensible and constructive discussion of the issues involved but to do this effectively they need to look outwards and involve parents, community leaders, employers, and the welfare services in their discussions. The implications of doing this: closer links with the community, more say for the parents, better attempts to understand and respond constructively to the criticisms which communities have of schools, open up a critique of the system that may prove unacceptable. On the one hand the traditionalist will be wary of the speed and nature of change of the schools. On the other, there is a growing antagonism to any attempt to use schools and the teachers as a palliative for what some people see as a deep pathological situation in our society.

Much of this uncertainty is reflected in teacher education where, in any event, helping new recruits to develop the skill and confidence with regard to control is one of the most difficult tasks. To be effective a teacher needs personal qualities not easily categorized and not identical in each individual, but adding up to a personality which thrives in the teaching situation. Teacher education, therefore, is as much about self-awareness and personal development as it is about skill. Most student teachers begin with strong anxieties about classroom control and need to test themselves in practical situations with the chance to get out honourably if skill and confidence do not develop. Sensitive guidance helps but, in the end, every teacher has to find his own methods. Good supervision not only involves giving practical help and monitoring standards, but also providing sensitive support when things go wrong. Teaching practice with 3B is likely to lead to much deeper levels of self-discovery than any academic examination! Unfortunately teacher education has become increasingly subject to a two-way stretch between the changing needs of the classroom and the pressure for graduate status. The study of Psychology and Sociology provides a valuable theoretical frame in which to consider the problem of maintaining discipline but in the form in which universities validate these subjects they do not adapt easily to offering practical help in organizing a crowded classroom or motivating an unwilling pupil.

Nor do the selection requirements of two A levels help. Experience, maturity and personality are vital factors in gaining children's confidence, but they now appear secondary to academic requirements. Good teacher education requires an effective blend of theory and practice, particularly where discipline is concerned, but it is very difficult to overcome the discrepancy between the highly cognitive study demanded by conventional examinations and the all-round blend of understanding, sympathy, and commitment, as well as intelligence, needed to organize and teach.

Ideally, there should be a mutually supporting process of professional development with classroom teachers and college tutors working together. Whatever aids and simulations colleges develop, sustained experience with good practising teachers is essential, particularly in a period of rapid change. Yet this experience depends heavily upon the goodwill and commonsense of those involved, to overcome the institutional barriers which divide colleges from schools and theory from practice: different salary scales and terms of service; hierarchical assumptions about status and levels of work, legal problems, local authority boundaries, let alone the technicalities of travel and timetables.

Prejudice is easily aroused between front line and training institutions in any field. But given the changes now facing schools and the diversity of response to the emotive and controversial questions of discipline and control, the need to build greater confidence and cooperation between training and reality is greater than ever. Attempts to do this are on the increase: teacher tutors, staff exchanges, joint appointments, joint involvement in course designs, special links between associate schools and colleges and school-based training. But there is a need for the validating bodies to recognize the importance of more structured cooperation and for the authorities to find the will and resources to achieve it.

At the same time training institutions have begun, albeit haltingly, to follow more practical responses to improving management and control within schools. Thus there is a growing emphasis upon internal efficiency and the essentials of good classroom management: understanding how to make and sustain good relationships, the thorough preparation of relevant materials: competence in subject matter, clarity in presentation, an enthusiasm for the task and empathy for the recipients.[1] But whilst the mechanics are important they can only be put into effect by committed and confident people who have a clear understanding of what is happening to and what is expected of schools and the conflicting perspectives involved.

Many student teachers still come straight into teaching from predominantly middle-class backgrounds and it is essential to give them the chance to gain a broader understanding of the context in which they have to work: to empathize with the restrictions of cramped housing conditions, to understand the insecurity of labouring jobs. It is only by being sensitive to such conditions and their causes that teachers can gain the confidence of the pupils and parents who are most likely to react against school. Additionally, by using such experience students can give personal meaning to their academic studies and sensible scrutiny to the ideological arguments for different forms of action in bringing about change.[2] To some extent efforts to select candidates with broader experience or to arrange for experience in other forms of work prior to teaching all help, whilst in-service training offers a further opportunity, but in the end it is not just the experience but the ability to use it that will count. In attempting to provide this experience, teacher education institutions begin to face the same dilemmas as schools about neutrality to change.

Like other agents of control – the police, managers in industry and the social services, the schools face the growing emphasis upon human rights and individual development which has created a much greater expectation of freedom and a general lessening of effective social disapproval. Children, like factory workers and social welfare clients, have become much more conscious of their rights and also much more knowledgeable about the world. Within the school this means that pupils expect more relaxed control, more consideration as individuals, and to 'see sense' in what they are asked to do.

The schools are not alone in this. The Royal Marines, for instance, recognize that new recruits have much greater confidence and understanding of the world and that young officers consequently have a much more demanding task in establishing their authority which has to be based more and more upon personal competence rather than any appeal to past expectations.

Yet, whilst schools seek to respond to these internal pressures they also have to respond to increasing external control. This in itself tends to restrict flexibility, but more significantly it reflects the conflict and uncertainty in our society, witness the different viewpoints raised during the Great Debate and by the Taylor Committee, and whilst economic performance fails to meet expectations such conflict is likely to increase.

Schools stand at the centre of this conflict. As formal agencies of care, selection and learning they influence the reasoning of their pupils and to that extent control them. Notwithstanding arguments about academic freedom, neutrality and child-centredness more and more people are becoming aware of the way in which schools are inevitably bound up in the subtle process with which power and influence are manipulated within democratic societies. Current reactions vary according to the particular interests of the group concerned and its strength of voice. However, when all the shouting is over it is not so much the understandable pattern of change in teacher–pupil relations taking place in the majority of schools that should cause concern as the growing rejection of formal education by significant groups in our society who feel the schools are failing them. In the run down inner cities, on the poorer housing estates, these problems are now acute, and symptoms are being felt in other areas. Some schools recognize this and are responding by trying to build better relationships with the communities they serve, to discuss more openly what they are trying to do and to gain confidence on as wide a base as possible.

This approach offers a constructive way forward but, at the same time, it begs questions, for whilst schools must seek sensible solutions to their present difficulties they are, by the very nature of the functions they carry out, very sensitive indicators of fundamental economic and political problems, and these cannot be solved by institutions of education alone.

Notes

1 A very useful summary of this approach can be found in *Classroom Management and Control*: the product of a working party chaired by Prof. E. C. Wragg at Nottingham University School of Education.

2 An example of this approach is reflected in the work of two Church colleges, St Mark and St John, and Ripon York St John who, with the help of the Gulbenkian Foundation, have established courses of community experience for teachers. This is being evaluated by Dr John Raynor of the Open University and a report will be published in the near future.

2 The disciplinary function of the head

Bernard Baxter

Headmaster, Gosforth High School, Newcastle-upon-Tyne

'The discipline of the school' is peculiarly, inescapably and at all times the concern of the head. Whatever tiers of responsibility are created, however much line delegation is practised, he* remains invested with a dominant role in the definition and implementation of rewards and punishments. Most heads would accept nothing less: one *hears* of schools where the head is said to be 'a figurehead and a gentleman' or perhaps a feeble appeaser, while a deputy exercises a 'hatchet-man' function. But these stories probably owe more to myth than reality (why should the deputy suppress them?) and in any case such a situation can hardly be an acceptable long-term arrangement. Indeed, the head is quite rightly held responsible by his employing LEA and governors for establishing and maintaining an ordered regime; and a new head very rapidly becomes aware of just how interested his staff are in his interpretation of and performance in his 'discipline' role – after all, their personal effectiveness, conditions of work and satisfaction in the job are significantly affected by his general philosophy of social control and by the way he handles particular issues. One of the early, and crucial, discoveries of headship is the extent to which the expectations and preferences of others (staff, parents, secretaries, caretaker, even pupils!) seek to limit and define his own view of the role. And there is a distinct likelihood that if the new head does not become absolutely the figure others wish him to be, he can all too easily slip into a compromise position between their pressures and his own ideals.

Like so much in education, heads have changed: compared with the old days one simply doesn't know where one is with them any more. My old grammar school head was entirely predictable: bramble-tweed suited and fustian gowned, he was a benevolent dictator, remote from the pupils, civil to the staff, likely to say no to any request that moved a hairsbreadth from established procedure, caning a few boys most days, moral and judicious in his public utterances – somewhat feared and generally respected. (But most teachers were archetypes in those days anyway.) Now it is fashionable to talk of 'models' of headship. There is the 'autocratic' who centralizes power in his own hands and rules by edict; the 'consultative' who sets up multifarious committees but retains for himself the power of veto; the 'democratic' who abdicates from decision-

* Please read the female alternative throughout.

13

making and puts all issues to a majority vote. And no doubt others. Like all cartoon characters these are amusing because sufficiently lifelike for staff to identify their own head in one guise or another, and sufficiently oversimplified for no one to take them too seriously. Similarly, current jargon has it that there is a 'continuum' running from anarchic permissiveness (on the Left, of course) to rigid formalism on the Right along which heads are strung out like so many battered beads according to their own schooling and subsequent prejudices or predilections. All grist to the mill of those para-educationists who don't have to soil their vocabularies with the actual job – and even the most experienced head talking to staff or parents or other heads – or anybody – is likely to be confronted with the miraculous capacity of words to mean only what the listener chooses to hear.

Headship is, in fact, an intensely pragmatic occupation, and not least where discipline is concerned.

A teacher reports a pupil to you for insolence, adding that he never has difficulties of this sort in the normal way, but this lout has cloven hooves and a tail and is beyond redemption. Even before you investigate the incident complained of, you know that this teacher is not one of those on your staff who has the gift of automatic control (that blend of experience, projection of innate authority, and simple liking for all sorts of people frequently analysed but never yet synthesized for injection into all new teachers). You also know that he would be surprised if anyone suggested that his discipline was less than perfect, and that he expects you to view the incident in the same outraged proportions as it looms before him. The idea that he hasn't necessarily handled the situation well, or that the boy may have a reasonable defence, will either not have occurred to him or will appear irrelevant in his world-picture: here the head figures as a *deus ex machina* striking humility and repentance into the heart of the miscreant, contriving further to extend these feelings to every other pupil who witnessed the episode and before whom the teacher feels he has lost face and ensuring that nothing of the sort will be allowed to happen again.

A sufficiently commonplace story, but it serves to lead into the heart of the discipline issue.

First the definition of the problem. It is very difficult to know, and perhaps not very profitable to enquire, whether children's behaviour is worse now than it was in the past. There are too many variables to make comparisons valid. But certainly we can define the trends and problems of our own time. Nationally there are areas of grave social disadvantage; everywhere there is a hard core, a tiny minority, of very difficult anti-socials. They concentrate mainly, but not universally, in inner-city areas where poverty, large families, broken marriages, bad or ill-designed housing, inadequate play facilities, the sterility of concrete, overcrowding and vice warp the moral, emotional and physical development of children. Generally parental control is very much less than it was, and is surrendered at an earlier stage in children's adolescence. In view of the 'pop' decibel count, it is hard to call it a silent revolution, but earlier physical maturity, less parental presence in the home (both parents working during the day and evening, more outlets for mass adult socializing), more money and rapid commercial exploitation of the teenage goldmine, a greater eroticism in teenage entertainment, a bureaucratization of crime enabling more people to be taken to court for breaking an ever-increasing number of rules – these and a host of other factors have created some of the problems inherent in compulsory education between five and sixteen.

So there are children physically and verbally violent, destructive and vandalistic, bored and frustrated, self-assertive and anti-authoritarian; just as there are children intelligent and enquiring, diligent and committed, friendly and cooperative. Some are most of these things at different times and in varying degrees. Many reflect their parents' attitudes and characteristics much more than those parents might think.

Potentially all the anti-social behaviour patterns discernible in society at large walk in through the school gates. In fact, relationships within the school environment (particularly when schools are functioning successfully as social units) are to a very great extent cooperative and cheerful because the vast majority of schools and school teachers always have been and still are keen on orderly behaviour and good at maintaining it. More teachers than ever before, whether or not formally so designated, see a pastoral concern as a necessary and important part of their jobs; social, psychiatric and medical services interact much more successfully with schools, and both with the law, than in the past.

What then do a head and his staff do about discipline? Two things are basic: to establish a system of social control that is liberal without being ineffective and to ensure that it is understood by all parties contracted to it; to encourage the growth of a total attitude or ethos which creates positive values rather than pessimism and faction.

All schools develop a formal 'pastoral care' system – whether it be 'horizontal' based on years or 'vertical' based on houses or a mixture of both. In either system, however good the year or house head (a remarkable breed to whose expertise the social stability of education is heavily indebted), the role of the form tutor is crucial since the strength of the system is tested most rigorously at this furthest point from the centre. Form tutors exert more direct daily influence on their group of pupils than anyone else in the pastoral chain: the smooth running of the school's administration and the health of its social intercourse depend heavily on their understanding of the functions delegated to them, the extent of their agreement with the general policies of the school, and the energy they devote to this aspect of their work. It is thus a most important function of the head's role to ensure adequate briefing of form tutors, and to establish consultative processes which enable them to pass on to colleagues their close knowledge of the changing circumstances, attitudes, health and social competence of members of their group. Too often form

tutors are the skivvies of the educational system, lumbered with un-
exciting chores – prising the termly sports contribution out of an unwilling clientele, engaging in running skirmishes over what is and is not
acceptable dress, organizing direct labour forces to pick up litter and
reduce graffiti. Then when something worthy of their professionalism
comes along, a more senior member of the hierarchy usurps it. It is thus
good practice and good sense to involve form tutors and make use of their
informed judgments regularly – for instance in asking them to take the
lead at staff discussions on pupils' progress by introducing the names of
pupils who worry them or deserve praise, and preparing for this by
meeting them beforehand to decide criteria for bringing forward particular names (should this meeting discuss the average for a change, the
ones who are usually passed over without comment?) or asking them to
prepare data to establish which pupils are apparently underachieving.
Form tutors can usefully sit in on fifth-year individual family interviews
to discuss careers or staying on to the sixth form and senior staff will often
be able to rely heavily on their advice in pitching the tone of the interview
correctly. They should certainly help to give advice when pupils make
option choices, and a head or deputy to whom a behavioural issue has been
referred will often find that the form tutor can supply invaluable background information.

Involvement of form tutors in these and many other ways is certainly
time-consuming but tends to produce mutual understanding and better
decisions, and is basic to the discipline of the school in its widest sense.

Side by side with the pastoral system is the academic structure, and
here again it is the teacher in the classroom hour by hour through the
school day who has the best chance to be sensitive to the warning signals
of distress, boredom, excitability that show – for whatever cause –
incipient behavioural problems. In large schools where staff meet colleagues irregularly or in splinter tea-making groups rather than frequently
in the main staffroom, it is vital to establish regular discussion meetings
which review the progress and development of all pupils in the school
group by group through the academic year. These meetings can be
overdone, too, in frequency and length, and it is good managerial practice to define very carefully the scope and purpose of particular meetings
so that staff come prepared to discuss the matter in question, are held to
the point by good chairmanship, and are made aware of decisions flowing
from them.

Shared knowledge of pupils, and a sense of one's colleagues' interaction
with them, can only produce better understanding leading to improved
relationships and more sensitive handling of behavioural problems. Thus
the discipline of the school is closely involved with management techniques.

In theory the twin pyramids – pastoral and academic (which, of course,
are mutually dependent and only clash when good management breaks
down) – are well capable of exercising social control. Where many

systems fall short however, is in the failure of all in the system to understand fully everyone else's role.

Most misdemeanours in a school ought to be dealt with on the spot by the nearest teacher, whether that is the teacher in the classroom, the tutor in the form room, the duty member in the corridor, or any teacher anywhere at any time. And they can be dealt with without resort to formal sanctions – a word to quieten, an instruction to move on, an admonition of appropriate sharpness. Far too often, of course, one's colleagues walk past a group they ought to have a word with and fail to notice behaviour that ought to be checked – or, at least, some are much more conscientious about such matters than others. One doesn't wish to have staff for ever chivvying pupils, but the exercise of professional judgment in when to make a quiet point to pupils ought clearly to be part of the life-style of all teachers: it is also the area in which a head is most likely to feel that matters are getting away from him, because it is exceedingly difficult to achieve consistency of attitude throughout an entire staff. Traditionally, schools decide on a set of 'rules', and it is these that staff agree to enforce consistently. However, rules are unfortunately generally linked with sanctions ($x=y$; specified misbehaviour =designated punishment), and it is my argument that where this philosophy obtains then on too many occasions minor matters escalate into more serious confrontations. I don't personally find sets of rules very useful. There is one necessary rule only: pupils are to behave at all times in a civilized way; if they don't they must be checked. And that checking in most cases need not involve any formal punishment. Thus tightness of control combined with lightness of touch is the norm to be aimed for.

Only where misbehaviour is more extreme or persistent, or where the authority of staff is deliberately challenged do we need to think in terms of sanctions, and the most useful approach then is to have a clearly understood referral system. This reflects the pyramid of responsibility in a school. If referrals are consistently made direct to the head over relatively minor matters, not only is his time unduly eroded but his most useful function – to be seen to be the ultimate court of appeal – is rendered less effective. Very often a strong form tutor who has built up a personal relationship with members of his group can deal adequately with an incident involving a member of staff with whom the pupil concerned doesn't often come into contact. Or a matter arising in the classroom can usefully be referred to the teacher's head of department. Beyond that, there is the year or house head, whose teaching commitments are very properly reduced, precisely because he will need to deal with a variety of personal problems; and then the deputy heads; finally the head.

The values of a properly established referral system are that staff and pupils know that there are levels of the structure at which matters of varying degrees of importance can be dealt with; recurrent offenders work their way up the system as their nuisance value increases; a simple matter that escalates is seen not to get out of hand but to assume a different level of importance and to be dealt with by the appropriate person. And, of course, a matter referred to the next level is likely to be dealt with more objectively and coolly, with the full facts about it systematically put together. Thus the head teacher dealing with a serious matter knows that it is probably of some long standing, has accumulated a case-history, and has failed to respond to lower levels of sanction. In any sensibly organized system, parents will have been contacted and involved at year or house head level and will also be aware that there is some substantial background to the matter. In this case the length of the chain is its strength.

This is not to suggest, of course, that the head should never deal with smaller matters: he has numerous roles, but if he is sensible he will regulate his involvement in them. Like other members of staff he walks along corridors and goes out to local shops – and in doing so deals on the spot, like them, with minor misdemeanours; he has a regular teaching commitment (or ought to and with some of the least amenable groups) and exercises the controlling skills of the teacher in the classroom – being thereby constantly reminded that it is one thing to play high court judge with an offender on particular occasions, and quite another to rub along with a group of pupils daily and weekly through the year. He also knows favourite congregation points and on occasions deliberately looks behind the sports hall and into the lavatories: he may be thought of by staff as perpetually seated in his study, but it ought not to be – and is worth demonstrating not to be – true.

However, even the best devised referral system is far from a tidy package, since there is a significant difference between individual members of staff and their capacity to deal with situations: what to one is a matter easily settled in passing may be beyond the scope of another. Any treatise on discipline must face the fact of the teacher whose discipline is inadequate. Nearly all beginning teachers have problems (which most of them soon overcome), no doubt, and in a well-organized school, departmental and year/house heads ought to have a clearly delegated responsibility to monitor the progress of junior staff – indeed, heads of department, in particular, are usually very anxious to do so in the interests of the general effectiveness, health and prestige of their subject. But it is the failure of established teachers which is the true worry. Sometimes a change of school, or of age-range of pupils, can enable a teacher ineffective in one situation to become happily competent in another; but it is sadly true that there is a proportion of teachers whose control falls below the high level necessary for successful teaching and that these teachers do not improve (to the detriment of the school they are in, and their own personal happiness). It is not a matter usually to which a particular head can find a satisfactory solution, however strenuously he seeks to ameliorate the problem. Furthermore, one weak teacher creates tensions which are not confined to his particular classroom but ripple right through the school. We have a right to expect, and a duty to ensure, that the falling birthrate at least results in a more careful screening of entrants to teaching, and a much more rigorous oversight of the probationary period before he or she is accepted as an absolute member of the profession.

'But,' says the questioner at every meeting, 'even if I accept your general thesis about discipline, what do you actually *do* with the hard-core recalcitrant pupil? What, come to that, do you *do* with any pupil who is a significant discipline problem?'

I do not personally believe that the traditional sanctions are the answer. Some people still seem to be seeking the ultimate deterrent: only give us sufficiently powerful sanctions, they say, and discipline problems will go away. Not so. Corporal punishment, detention systems, idiot lines and essays (which make the task of the English staff harder than it is already) have little relevance for those teachers who seek to treat teenagers as emerging adults and give them real standards, and who have a compassionate understanding of the difficulties and pressures of growing up, family and peer-group stresses, the limited personal resources of some individuals. Beating children is abhorrent in itself, but also – as extracts from those unconsciously hilarious documents School Punishment Books amply demonstrate – ineffective in changing behaviour. But this is familiar ground and, I believe, very generally accepted: the whole ethic of society is moving away from belief in the right and duty of the establishment to chastise and towards the necessity of training the young, the weak and the misguided to take their place in a free and civilized community through self-discipline – a conscious effort to advance positive standards, and convince the transgressor that because what he has done is against the well-being of society or some of its members it is ultimately against his own wellbeing. This is sometimes represented by the hardliners as weakness, but as society grows very rapidly more complex and its members ever more mutually interdependent it is the only way – short of recurrent pogroms – to avoid social disaster.

'But what do you *do*?' First, find a proper perspective. Within school (and within society at large) there are very very few utterly intransigent individuals: the great majority are happy in and cleave to an ordered community; of those who rebel, most do so occasionally rather than as a way of life; very few are unbiddable. The minority make the problems loom large because they require a relatively enormous expenditure of time and effort compared with the majority who conform. Obsessed with the problems in our own school we don't see the relativity of the whole situation. For every school its worst problems seem to be worst in an absolute sense, when in fact many schools have remarkably few problems of any order of severity while some have genuinely many more and some of these much more intense. (It is tempting to argue that schools in generally the latter category make less noise and work very hard to overcome their problems, while some in the former category wring their collective hands and cry woe while doing much less, and indeed I believe this frequently to be so – but it doesn't help to generalize.)

Secondly, seek to change attitudes and behaviour.

Many of our problems are of our own making. Thus the curriculum is at the heart of the school, no less at the heart of its discipline, and if the curriculum has little to offer lower ability pupils boredom, truancy and anti-social behaviour are predictable. This is not the argument sometimes advanced for a curriculum that is in a facile sense 'interesting' and 'relevant'. The school leaving age was raised to sixteen – and quite rightly so – in order to educate more pupils to a higher level than when they left at fifteen, and that implies an insistence on the acquisition of knowledge and skills some of which may be directly useful in earning a living but more in coping adequately with living in a complicated bureaucracy and raising the quality of leisure. We still tend to cherish the most able (who have the absolute right to be extended educationally to their personal limits) and spend too few of our resources, or misdirect them, in the education of the less able. CSE which started out so hopefully, and has indeed achieved so much, is in danger of becoming an opiate, a means of placating the average and less able by giving them an apparent something but in fact almost nothing. Thus it is a discipline issue urgently to research and rethink our curriculum provision for those of lower ability.

In our school structures we demonstrate over and over again to these pupils that they are held in lesser esteem. What leadership and service opportunities do we give them? How carefully do we assess the demoralizing effect of low marks, negatively critical reports, 'no-hope' sink sets or bands? Thus sensitivity to these issues is crucial to the discipline of the school also. I was very impressed by a scheme operated in one school I was associated with by which 'reinforcement' education was carefully timetabled to allow withdrawal from normal mixed ability lessons not merely for remedial help but for a range of purposes – to extend the most able or to concentrate on a failure of understanding identified in some part of the syllabus. In particular withdrawal was used to take the disruptive, the attention seekers, and the extremely lazy out of normal classes for a week or a fortnight with the intention that normal classes could proceed in the interests of the education of the majority, while the few were given individual guidance and helped to re-establish themselves with a view to going back more successfully into their regular teaching groups.

Thirdly, when a pupil presents a serious case of indiscipline, work with all those who can help. The most important of these are parents, with whom the school is inevitably in partnership. It is a feature of our society that parents often feel isolated and helpless in coping with a rebellious child whom they can see sliding into trouble at school and with the law. If teachers feel that an ill-organized and pressurized society leaves them with many more problems than they used to have, so too do parents who often feel that nobody is reinforcing them in their efforts to bring up their children. This is partly a matter of communication: parents may well be faced by the school with a fairly serious problem without having been made aware that it was developing over a period of time; they may be resentful of a school whose systems they do not understand; they may have expectations about the school's role that are unrealistic or unreasonable. But they are the school's greatest potential asset and however hard-pressed our lives it is difficult to quantify the value of the time spent in contact with parents.

Mutual suspicion between school and the psychiatric service and the social welfare services is, I hope, disappearing. They have a great deal of expertise, and know very well that difficult cases mend slowly. A good working relationship with them can be extremely valuable. Many local education authorities have Special Services sections whose potential is often far from realized as a result of insularity in schools and an understandable but misguided desire to keep County Hall at bay. The police, who have a difficult job to do themselves, can be extremely valuable allies, and I am sure relations between school and GPs are in far too primitive a stage.

Discipline is not a matter of easy answers – we should all have got it right by now if it were. It is a matter of pursuing an overall philosophy in offering positive standards to pupils and seeking to change unacceptable behaviour by persuasion rather than force. It is a matter not only for the head, but for the head working in a team of which his whole staff and many people outside the school are or ought to be members. It is inextricably linked not only with the overt curriculum but also all those factors of attitude and ethos which we call the hidden curriculum.

This chapter previously appeared in *Management and Headship in the Secondary School*, edited by Arnold Jennings, published by Ward Lock Educational in 1977.

3 An Inspector calls

Joan Dean
Chief Inspector, Surrey LEA

John Andrews was nearing the end of his first year of teaching English in a comprehensive school in a small town in the south of England. He was able, energetic and enthusiastic and had started on his career with a feeling of mission to inspire his pupils with his own love of literature and enjoyment of writing. Now after eight months he was aware of the difficult task teachers faced and of his own inadequacy so far as the less able and most difficult pupils were concerned. Although there had been high spots in the year, where pupils in the top sets had responded to him with real interest, he was conscious of not yet being sufficiently in control of the less able sets actually to teach them very much. He had also begun to question what he was offering them and its relevance to their needs.

Mary Markham was a well-qualified teacher of mathematics. She left her Oxbridge College with a good degree for a post in a girls' grammar school in a pleasant country town and since she was not particularly ambitious, had stayed there for twenty-five years until the school was reorganized as a mixed comprehensive for 11–16-year-olds. At no time had she been a strong or even a good teacher. She was at her best with able sixth formers and had had some trouble with the third form in the grammar school. The four years since reorganization seemed like a bad dream. She was unable to control children adequately at any level and with sixth-form work removed and very little examination work, she found herself with very few opportunities to do the work she could do best. Every class contained children who seemed uncontrollable and rude and who appeared to inhabit a world as far removed from her own as a jungle tribe. She saw no way of coping with the situation, dreaded Mondays and longed for Friday night.

Sheila Blount was Deputy Head of a First School. She was a competent able teacher who could manage any age group with ease. It was a long time since she had met a child with whom she could do nothing and she was astonished when Stuart, a five-year-old, was admitted to her class and before the first morning was out had proceeded to smash everything in sight. Attempts to restrain him verbally fell on deaf ears and when she went to hold him, he kicked, bit and scratched her to the point where she had to send another child for help.

Later investigation revealed that Stuart was the illegitimate child of a teenage mother who had walked out on her own family and sought the support of a succession of 'uncles'. Stuart was a liability to her, but she had refused to have him adopted. She frequently went out leaving him tied to a table leg in a locked room. When she left him free to roam the house, he would often attack the latest boyfriend and in consequence, she restricted him more and more and in an attempt to quiet him, frequently used physical violence. At five, he was virtually uncontrollable.

In the classes of John Andrews and Mary Markham there were also children who seemed uncontrollable. Stephen was a case in point. He was one of a family of four second-generation West Indians. Long before he entered school he had encountered colour prejudice and he had the misfortune at a very early stage, to meet a teacher who ridiculed his way of talking. By eight, he shared the conviction of his older brothers that school was not worth having and nothing which happened later changed that view.

Maria at fifteen was the eldest of six. Her mother had deserted the family when she was thirteen and from then on she was forced to assume responsibility for her younger brothers and sisters. This task she did reasonably well, but it took all her spare time and she was often tired. School offered a welcome break from the responsibilities of home. It became a place where she could behave like a child among children. She avoided work whenever possible and used her home responsibilities as an excuse.

These children are not untypical of many in our schools today. They pose problems for those who teach them and often for the community outside the school. The teachers too, may have problems and there are both teachers and children who are in the first place, the victims of circumstance, the casualties of our society. This is not to deny that perhaps Mary Markham could do more to help herself; that Stephen and Maria were often to blame for their behaviour, but to note that very often the problems are complex in origin and unlikely to be solved by any simple panacea. While their complexity must not be used as an excuse for doing nothing about them, any consideration of discipline in schools or in the community must start by recognizing the difficulties.

Many of those reading this book will be looking for answers to questions about how a parent, a teacher, a school or a community deals with the kinds of problems described above. The answers, like the questions, are complex and often come down to the relationship between particular individuals.

In recent years, many things have made the task of the school and the teacher more difficult. The sanctions which schools were once able to apply, and which were generally supported by parents and the community, are no longer accepted as appropriate by some sections of the school population and the public. The raising of the school leaving age has changed the situation from one in which the sixteen-year-olds were in school because they wanted what school could give them, to one in which some are there perforce and very unwillingly.

At the same time we need to get these problems into perspective. If one reads the right wing press and never visits a school, one might be forgiven for thinking that all our schools were blackboard jungles and that the entire system was breaking down. This is not the case. One can visit school after school and meet polite, hard working and orderly pupils; go into classroom after classroom and see teachers teaching and children learning. The vast majority of our schools are orderly and disciplined places where most pupils learn effectively. Most classrooms are places where the teacher is in control. Most children in school want to do the right thing and win approval and want to learn, and almost all teachers at the beginning of their careers experience some problems of discipline. Skill in controlling children in groups is one which only a very few people seem to have from the start. Most acquire it during their first year of teaching. A few take longer but still make the grade and a few never acquire it. Some of these may leave teaching but a few remain unhappy individuals who are a thorn in the flesh to their colleagues.

In order to find answers to the questions posed we need to consider fairly carefully what we mean by discipline, whether in school or outside it. What sorts of people do we want our children to be? Do we really want them to have ideas, to question what is established, to be inventive and creative and critical, able to reason and argue and think things through? Teachers have for many years regarded these as proper ends for education, but the trouble is that once you encourage people to ask questions and to think critically, you have to be prepared for the possibility that they will question established values and practices. Certainly it would seem that as never before, young people are questioning what happens to them at school and in some cases they are demonstrating very clearly their non-acceptance of the values of the school.

Another facet of this problem is that our society has been changing very considerably in recent years. We have many new members of British society, who are bringing with them different ideas and a different morality from our own. Cheaper travel has meant that many people have had at least some opportunity to see other countries and other societies, if only from a hotel balcony. The world has also become more crowded and people more mobile, so that the constraints which control the members of a small community where people are interdependent and cannot afford to deviate too far, no longer operate.

Present-day young people are growing up into a confusing world where choices and decisions have to be made all the time with few of the rules which seemed so self-evident to our parents and grandparents. Sexual morality has changed, whether we like it or not, with the advent of the pill and it is difficult for the older generation of women conditioned against sex outside marriage to understand how it feels to be able to enjoy sex without fear of pregnancy. The girl who has intercourse with a number of boyfriends may have strong views about right and wrong in relationships but her morality is very different from past morality. It is difficult for an older generation operating under different rules to accept that she is not being self-indulgent in spite of her conscience, but may genuinely not regard her behaviour as wrong and that she too has clear rules which govern her behaviour which are different from theirs.

There are of course, many things which most civilized communities regard as wrong, although it is salutary to reflect that for almost every moral rule we have, there may somewhere be a community for whom the opposite rule holds good. Most of us condemn violence and vandalism as negative as well as painful, yet there is no doubt that at least some of those who act violently are as untroubled of conscience or even feel as righteous as the teacher who canes a boy, the warder who locks up the prisoner or the soldier who kills an enemy. Our views of the rights and wrongs of a particular piece of violence depend to a large extent on where we stand, the values we hold and on the size and standing of the group which supports us and to which we see ourselves as belonging. The teacher caning the boy may do so with the support of the boy's parents and of the school community. Once the community withdraws support, this particular act of violence becomes unacceptable and may bring social disapproval on the teacher.

Each society and group within the larger society controls its members in various ways and has expectations of them. Society generally expects that schools will set standards for children and see that they are upheld and particular schools do this in particular ways. But pupils spend more hours out of school than in school and the groups that they belong to out of school and the peer groups in school may have very different expectations and values. Thus the peer group may expect violence and a flouting of established authority from its members and those who aspire to be part of such a group may be under some pressure to demonstrate their solidarity with the group. This kind of solidarity very frequently operates within schools and classrooms and success in teacher baiting and going against the values of the school staff may well be seen as a membership test. Any useful consideration of discipline must involve some understanding of this phenomenon and a recognition of the strength of the pressure on some young people to conform to the norms of the group.

The dictionary definitions of the word discipline come into two broad categories. There are those definitions concerned with the maintenance of order and those concerned with a discipline as a branch of learning.

Order may be maintained from without or from within an individual or a group. The young child, because he is weak and helpless and needs the care of others, has to accept the discipline imposed by others and all of us need to do this to some extent throughout life. As the child grows however, he learns to discipline himself to achieve ends he sees as worthwhile and part of the task of the adult is to help him to see ahead and achieve the necessary self-discipline to meet his goals. Some of this self-discipline will be achieved by the process of conditioning. The child does as the adult wishes and is rewarded by praise and approval, so that he associates the action with the reward and comes to regard it as good in itself. He therefore continues to act in this way even when there is no adult present.

This process continues to operate for all of us throughout life. A teacher who wishes to change a child's behaviour will do it most easily by identifying the behaviour required in some detail and rewarding in some way each small step towards it. Some teachers in special education with pupils posing very severe problems of behaviour have achieved remarkable success with this process of behaviour modification. The trouble is often that it is difficult to spend sufficient time with any individual to make the process really effective. It is also often difficult to identify the necessary small steps.

As the child grows he meets other forms of discipline; those of the material world and of ideas. The material world operates according to unchanging laws which we gradually learn and this learning enables us to predict and control our environment. The young child exploring his environment learns about the nature of water and earth and fire and materials and how to live safely with them. As he grows he will also learn to explore what can be done with materials like paint and clay and fabric and wood and to experience the discipline they impose.

There is also a discipline inherent in other areas of learning. Mathematics operates according to its rules; sentences follow rules of construction; history has rules about evidence and so on. This is really part of the other definition of the word discipline. Mathematics, language and history are 'disciplines' because they have an inherent order of their own to which those who study or use them must submit.

People are also controlled by the beliefs and ideas they hold. If, for example, you believe it to be wrong to hit someone else, you are likely to use that belief to govern your behaviour when you are angry. The discipline of beliefs and ideas is seen most clearly in religious behaviour, where what a person believes governs his behaviour in ways which might appear unlikely in other contexts.

We have already seen that in any group there will be a common acceptance of a set of values and expectations of behaviour and various kinds of social sanction which operate to keep the deviant in check. Members of a community usually have a number of things which are highly valued and others which are 'not done' and these views govern the members for much of the time because they accept these views and values and want to be part of the community. The problems arise when this accepted framework begins to be questioned and challenged, or when the framework needs to be extended or stretched to accommodate new groups. People who have lived under the discipline of an accepted framework for a long time sometimes find it difficult to accept that it must be a flexible and dynamic thing and they therefore resist pressures to change by becoming inflexible and rigid about the views they hold, insisting that these are the only possible or the only 'right' values.

A school is in some ways a rather special community, because of the immaturity of large numbers of its members and the assumptions we make about the nature of childhood and adolescence. We assume that children at school are not able to accept genuine responsibility in the real world and we do a good deal to protect them from learning from real life experience. Yet in more primitive communities quite young children are expected to act responsibly and it is hard to imagine when we look at a class of seven-year-olds, that it is not long since irresponsible and volatile children of this age were working long hours in factories where presumably they were obliged to behave in ways we now find very difficult to imagine. Perhaps part of the current difficulties in dealing with adolescents is that we don't rate highly enough the ability to be independent in living and learning or to take genuine responsibility and much school activity thus lacks the discipline inherent in the real-life situation.

A recent article in *Education* by Dudley Fiske, Chief Education Officer for Manchester described the pattern of work experience offered to some school children in East Germany. Each class in a secondary school spent an afternoon each week in a factory where they took over part of a production line and were responsible for the output and for reaching production targets. This would seem to have its own built-in discipline.

In a similar way, a group of people whether in school or elsewhere who work together to a common end accepted by them all as worthwhile, exercise a discipline on each other and no member of the group feels he can give less than his best because he will let down the group. This is perhaps most clearly seen on the games field, but is equally applicable to other work. In adult life a great deal of work involves this kind of interdependence, but school work tends to be individual rather than cooperative, and this would seem to be an area which could be profitably developed.

Schools by their nature are often forced to use artificial situations to teach children about the outside world. These inevitably lack the discipline present in the real-life context. Many schools could, with profit, become much more part of the community, using genuine opportunities for learning whenever possible. Unfortunately this is often very difficult to do without disturbing vested interests on the one hand and coming up against legislation on the other. One problem of the legislation that we have to protect children is that it protects them from the good as well as the bad. The ten-year-old who earned a few pence helping the milkman may well have been learning valuable lessons which he can no longer officially learn.

The discipline of a school depends upon an acceptance by teachers, parents and children of a common framework of values and expectations. The various groups involved in this will make the framework their own only if they have an opportunity to talk about and think through the aspects which are not usually part of their thinking. The fee-paying independent school has comparatively little need to do this since it can choose pupils who fit the framework of the head and staff and if necessary, ask those who do not fit to leave. The multicultural comprehensive needs to put a great deal of time and effort into doing it, because many of its members have frameworks of their own which are different from those of other pupils and from those of the head and staff. The comprehensive school like the elementary school before it, also has to accept virtually allcomers and is not in a position to reject those who don't fit in. It is perhaps worth noting here that there are important learning possibilities in hammering out such a framework, since it offers a lesson in community problem-solving. The comprehensive thus offers its pupils opportunities for social learning and for seeing life from other very different points of view which it is difficult to provide in a one-culture school. These opportunities need to be seen as advantages and grasped.

The framework within which a school may operate has formal and informal levels. At the formal level there will be recognized rules which may or may not be written and a recognized system of rewards and of dealing with breaches of discipline by referrals and sanctions of various kinds. This is a valuable support for teachers as well as children and is very necessary in a large school. In addition, there is an informal system which is not always made explicit and each new group of pupils needs to explore the rules and the boundaries which govern them. They try out how far a teacher will go, what they can do with impunity whatever the written rules may say, and what gets them into trouble as well as what brings praise and encouragement. They may discover that the rules which operated at home or in their previous school no longer operate at the next stage and it is sometimes the case that children get into trouble for doing what they were formerly encouraged to do. Generally they learn rapidly and become secure in their knowledge of the boundaries within which they are working and are supported by the framework of discipline in the school, but sometimes this process takes a long time partly because the school does too little to help new pupils to find the boundaries.

The framework within which a school operates will need a certain amount of renegotiation with each new group of parents and pupils and needs to be discussed with new teachers. It depends for its success on its acceptance by the large majority of the community whose support is needed in dealing with the minority. It is not really possible for a head and staff to maintain a framework of discipline if the majority of parents and pupils do not support them. There are far more pupils than teachers and the ability of any school to carry out the task which society requires of it, depends upon the willingness of the pupils to accept and profit by what is offered to them. It is the fear that large numbers of pupils will combine to rebel against the staff that makes large-scale indiscipline in a school frightening and emotionally exhausting. It is the task of the head and senior management of the school to evolve the kind of framework of discipline which is acceptable to the community and possible to maintain and to work to keep this position. This does not mean accepting low standards or adopting a do-as-you-please attitude. Very few parents or pupils want an undisciplined school in which little learning takes place. What they do want, however, is a school in which children are accepted and valued, whatever their background and whatever their potential; a school in which there is care for the individual, praise and recognition for honest effort as well as for achievement; opportunities to be challenged and stimulated; to fulfil potential and an opportunity to take responsibility and to learn.

What it also means is that the staff of any school should talk together about the aims of the school and how these are borne out in the way children are treated and are expected to behave. While it is obvious that in a large staff, there will be many differences in teacher expectation of pupils, it is, nevertheless important to achieve as much consistency as possible, so that everyone is clear what should and should not be allowed and so that there is to some degree a united front, with good support for the inexperienced, and an overall system which supports the aims and values of the school. This takes time to work out and needs time for its maintenanace.

In a similar way, each successive group of pupils and their parents need opportunities to talk about what the school is trying to do and what will be expected of children. This too takes time and time is one resource which cannot be extended. If time is not taken for such discussion, however, a great deal more time may be taken in dealing with those who flout rules and regulations laid down by others.

Where such attitudes and opportunities are missing, there is likely to be trouble, however firm the discipline. From time to time it is salutary to look at what has been offered to the pupils regarded as least able and those who are difficult and disruptive with these points in mind. It is still not unusual to find the least able in the worst accommodation and with the greatest turnover of teachers. Remedial work frequently attracts lower salaries than work in other departments and is often regarded as of comparatively low status. Pupils who are of low ability frequently get fewer opportunities for reasoning and thinking independently because they are not thought to be good at this. Consequently they may more often be expected to learn by rote than more able children and this makes learning less challenging and interesting. It does little to increase their ability to think and reason and little to increase their learning ability and confidence.

In a rather similar way we tend to offer opportunities for taking responsibility to those who have shown that they are able to use them, rather than those who need practice in being responsible.

Very few schools deliberately set out to discourage the least able and the most difficult, but it can be difficult with the current stress on examination results to maintain a level of recognition for effort and for the achievement of the less able which is sufficient to spur them on to fresh achievement.

A school is primarily a community for learning. Order and discipline are necessary preconditions for learning at every stage. The child joining a nursery class or the first five-year-old entering school must be controlled by others in a number of aspects of his daily life because as yet, he has only developed a limited ability to control himself for ends other than those which are of immediate importance to him. He is, however, often able to exercise very considerable self-discipline in his efforts to communicate and in his play because those activities are of deep emotional importance to him.

The good teacher of this age group will use this emotional drive to help the child to learn not only what he wants to learn himself, but what she, as a teacher representing society wants him to learn. She is thus able for at least some of the time to harness the self-discipline that he is already able to exercise. He will, in addition, be continually encountering the discipline of the material and cognitive world. He will learn what he can and cannot do, not because anyone says yes or no, but because things are as they are. Part of the task of the teacher in this context, is to help him to deal with this learning, developing control over the material world where this is possible and coming to terms with it where it is not.

Even at this stage the teacher will need to impose discipline in order to ensure the safety of the children in her care and in order to provide the necessary preconditions for learning. She is likely to use two ways of doing this. She will use the conditioning techniques of praising and rewarding the behaviour she wants and discouraging in various ways the behaviour she sees as undesirable. She is here using the child's need for praise and encouragement. She will also use the group of children to control the individuals within it. She will make comments like 'we do it this way' or 'we don't do that in this class' or she will single out those children who are doing the thing she wants for praise and recognition and those who are doing the wrong thing for adverse comment. Here she is using the child's need for acceptance to aid her in controlling the group. She will not only make these points explicitly in words, but by her tone of voice, gesture and facial expression will be continually communicating what she wants and what she doesn't want. Thus the child who is seeking the security of doing what the powerful adult wants, rapidly learns to read this unspoken communication which sets for him the boundaries of behaviour.

These aspects of discipline are common to all stages of education and at all stages teachers need to achieve the kind of balance using the self-discipline which comes from interest, the discipline which stems from conditioning and the interaction of group and individual, or to put it a different way, from using the child's need for acceptance, recognition and praise.

As the child grows, however, various developments take place. The conditioning of the early years will lead him to form habits which may or may not be helpful to learning. He also develops attitudes to school and to learning which may help or hinder him.

There is also development in what may be done because of the child's self-interest. He will still be motivated by the satisfaction of his emotional needs, but these become more complex and varied as children grow older. We have a tendency to ignore these needs in the later years of schooling, particularly for the more able, for whom education can often be a too cerebral business. All children and young people need the kinds of opportunities for emotional satisfaction offered by studies such as art, music, drama and the creative and imaginative aspects of English. It should not be forgotten, however, that studies like mathematics and science also have their inherent emotional satisfaction. What is needed is breadth and balance.

As the child grows he may increasingly find satisfaction in the content of his learning and may thus be disciplined by it and prepared to discipline himself in order to learn more. We sometimes forget that learning is an activity natural to human beings and consequently can and should be a satisfying and enjoyable activity for much of the time, which brings its own incentive to hard work. There is a power for learning in all of us which we are not always able to tap and there is no doubt that there is vastly greater potential in almost all children than we are able to develop at present.

A second incentive to learning which becomes very powerful at the secondary stage of education is that of public recognition of what has been learned in the form of examination success and later in successful employment. The trouble with the strength of this motivation is that it far too often stands in place of motivation by content and many young people are therefore led to value what they learn in terms of what it will do for them in terms of examination success and employment, rather than what it might do for them as people or by the intrinsic interest of what they are learning. In consequence those parts of the curriculum which are not examination orientated are often devalued and those pupils considered too poor as learners to win recognition through examination success are regarded as failures. It is perhaps not very surprising if they react against a value system which creates this situation and pose problems of discipline. The solution would seem to be firstly to create a curriculum which is seen by everyone to be interesting and worthwhile in its own right whether it offers examination success or not and to offer with it various other forms of public recognition of achievement. This is of course easier said than done, but is more often achieved by ESN(M) schools than secondary schools.

The point was made earlier that we do not rate highly enough the ability to be independent in living and learning and to take genuine responsibility. The Plowden Report spoke of children becoming 'agents in their own learning' and clearly the best learning at all stages involves this kind of involvement and the self-discipline which goes with it. The development of self-discipline requires increasing opportunities for a child to take responsibility for his learning. This means teaching him how to study, how to find out by observing, questioning and using books, how to organize himself, his work and time and giving him the chance to put this learning into practice. Many primary schools start this process but in the later years in the primary school and through the secondary school, the pressure for children to acquire content militates against any real development of independence in learning and the self-discipline which needs to go with it. Even in the sixth form we are only beginning to see the need for this and Colleges of Further and Higher Education and Universities are usually extremely critical of their students' lack of ability to study and to organize their own learning.

It is, of course, not very surprising that teachers are hesitant about taking the risks that an investment in teaching children to be independent learners involves. It needs to be a gradual development, with increasing responsibility offered year by year and there needs to be a general commitment to autonomy on the part of the majority of a staff. It is also not just a matter of providing periods for private study, but of identifying skills, and training children in their use, providing opportunities for their practice with supervision, eventually leading to independent learning. It needs a programme of planned development and evaluation and it should be a programme for all children. For as many sixteen-year-olds as possible, such a programme needs to have as a goal the ability to learn without a teacher. If we gave this higher priority in schools, we might well find that learning was in the long run more effective and that discipline problems were reduced.

The most important element in this is clearly the quality of the teacher. The good teacher may be able to stimulate and interest many children who are rejecting the values of school. On the other hand, he may be a very good teacher of the most able but may offer very little to the rest or the converse may be true. Although this is valuable there is less place for such teachers in schools now than formerly. What we need most at present is teachers who are able across the full range of ability.

Good teaching must of course involve the presentation of content in the context of the experience and interests of the learners. It must also involve very good organization and both of these sets of abilities will contribute to a teacher's ability to control children. It is, however, rather a chicken and egg situation, in that the presentation and organization may be useless without a measure of control.

The ability to control children in groups is in many ways a mysterious process. There are those who have difficulty with control but have much to teach and those who control children with ease but have little to offer them as well as teachers who have both. The ability to control children is sometimes found in the gentle and feminine of both sexes and is not invariably present in the tough and the masculine. One can see people who do all the wrong things and succeed and others who do all the right things and fail.

On the other hand, there is a good deal which is specific and can be learned. The difference between the good experienced teacher and the inexperienced is that the inexperienced teacher is often uncertain about what he should expect and this communicates itself to the children. The experienced teacher quickly sets the boundaries with comments like 'we do it this way' or 'no more than four people may use this equipment at the same time' or 'which of you can remember what you should do when the bell goes?' and so on. He may also indicate boundaries by tone of voice and gesture and by the way he arranges the environment and presents material. He anticipates possible misunderstandings and tries to organize it so that things go smoothly and so that work and explanation match the needs of the children. He is also quick to see and stop those who overstep the boundaries and continually scans the group, ready to intervene when necessary.

A lot of this behaviour has been acquired through trial and error and eventually becomes instinctive. You know that if you organize so that there are long periods of waiting, things will go wrong. You become adept at steering the troublemakers into the right seats and to the right work. You learn to scan the room while you are talking to an individual or a group and to gesture with your eyes. You learn to project very clearly and definitely what you are expecting and to make children very conscious of it. You also learn your own strengths and weaknesses, using the former and compensating for the latter.

None of this happens overnight and it is one of the problems of the isolated single-teacher classroom that the inexperienced teacher is cut off from opportunities to observe other teachers at work and so discover ways of dealing with problems. He may also be cut off from any professional feedback on his own performance as a teacher at a time when this would be very valuable indeed. Good team teaching situations offer a very useful learning opportunity for the inexperienced.

Any school wishing to establish a framework of good discipline would do well to provide opportunities for teachers to see each other at work and if they are willing, to discuss performance. It also needs to provide a good support system for the inexperienced and to make it clear that it is not a sign of weakness or failure to use it. Indiscipline in one class in a school affects other classes and if children are allowed to behave badly towards one teacher this may affect their attitudes towards others. Help needs to be near at hand and readily given to the inexperienced.

In considering a subject like discipline, it is important to remember that it is a means to an end and not an end in itself. The school in which teachers are men and women of vision as well as good practitioners, will have few problems of discipline if the teachers are able to communicate their own enthusiasm and excitement to the pupils.

We are at present suffering in education from a great deal of ill-informed criticism and a little which we accept as justified and valuable. The critics offer negative views apparently without even noticing the many good things taking place. This approach is known by teachers to be ineffective in helping pupils to improve. It is equally ineffective with teachers.

If we really want to move forward in education we must at all costs maintain and develop our vision of what education and society might be. There are many men and women of vision in our schools. They need our support and encouragement.

4 A middle-school viewpoint

Tom Gannon
Headmaster, Milefield School, Barnsley

Middle schools are newcomers to the educational scene and still thin on the ground, though geographically widely spread, in England at least. Will the practice of discipline in middle schools be different from that of other schools, i.e. the great majority, which cater for the middle years, but also contain within their age-groups either younger or older children? Before discussing this question it might be pertinent to consider the nature and practice of school discipline in general, and the rather selective and indeed somewhat naïve view of it held by the public, as against the overall professional standpoint of those who have to exercise it. Schools do vary significantly in terms of their social climate or 'atmosphere' irrespective of their differences in size, age-groups, curricular practices, geographical location, etc. This difference is indeed most apparent when a visitor to a number of schools is able to compare two which on all the counts mentioned above have greatly similar attributes. Wherein lies the difference is difficult to describe in words – similar or dissimilar schools – the visitor will leave with a more favourable impression of one as against another, will discount superficial yet very real advantages or disadvantages of site, size, age of buildings and so forth, and will seize instead on this seeming abstraction of 'tone' or climate to substantiate his judgment.

This property of tone or climate is by no means a vague or illusory element in the general appraisal of the character of a school – on the contrary – it seems to be a contributory factor in determining disciplinary policy, and in maintaining consistency of control. Where a suitable way of describing the 'climate' or character of a given school could be devised, it would probably illustrate in a realistic and cogent manner, the disciplinary policy within that school. Such an exercise would be most beneficial in helping to decide what was worth preserving from the current code of conduct in the school, and what might be profitably discarded. Internal, periodic assessments of this kind would be more illuminating than attempts to measure success or otherwise, in disciplinary policy, in terms of comparison with other schools of the same type. At the same time, obviously successful measures attained by other schools, especially in those where the same measurement systems had been carried out, would be considered for adoption.

The design of measurement systems to determine social climate has already been undertaken earlier in the decade by Finlayson (1970) and Finlayson et al. (1970–71) and details of their construction, validity, etc. are already published.[1] A lengthy description of their design patterns, etc. would be inappropriate here, but briefly they are based on the pupils' perceptions of the behaviour of their peers, teachers' perceptions of their colleagues' behaviour and further teacher perceptions of the attitudes and behaviour of those senior to them such as departmental heads, and heads of schools. When considered together the measurement of these perceptions gives a reasoned analysis of a school's social system, in the form of a 'School Climate Index', and by association, a survey and appraisal of the disciplinary policy adopted.

Such sophistication, an interpretation of discipline as a synthesis, something integral and corporate for a school, and each of its individual parts, seems far removed from the public preoccupation with discipline solely as an instrument of punishment or a deterrent. Regrettably, parts of the media too seem obsessed with this punitive aspect of discipline, especially with corporal punishment, and with its application or non-application in one sector of secondary education, the comprehensive school, rather than in any other state or private sector. Secondary teachers are thus brought to a realization that 'standards', another favourite media word, might have a different interpretation also, from the one they would place upon it. Consider for example, a comprehensive school in the Midlands, which has all the contributory elements almost to ensure what the media would regard as 'poor' discipline.

It is situated in the inner-city, built on two sites, one of which is a mile distant from the other, in very old buildings. It has something over 2,000 students on roll, more than 60 per cent of whom are from immigrant families. It has, in fact, an enviable social climate and correspondingly good discipline, a pleasant atmosphere of purposeful work and of accord between staff and students. It has, of course, behaviour problems, because of high rates of external delinquency, but the prevailing good order within counteracts the undesirable pressures from without. Such schools except rarely, and in a limited local sense, seem to escape the attention of the media, as do the efforts of the vast majority of schools, some of which have similar circumstances to overcome, unless an isolated example of unruly behaviour or 'plummeting' standards can be highlighted. The damaging effects of exterior patterns of behaviour or a school's efforts to nullify or mitigate them would, if similarly publicized, eventually bring about a diminution of anti-social or antipathetic modes of behaviour. Nowadays a school which struggles mightily to keep a protective cover of good disciplinary control over its pupils is rewarded with a blanket of silence at best, or a howl of obloquy when there is a temporary break in the pattern. The bitter fight for the good of the child, by teachers and welfare officers, against a horde of pernicious influences, some, ironically, media-inspired, is mainly an unpublicized and unsupported war, in which it should be a cause for wonder that so few battles are lost, given the seemingly intractable odds against. The contrast between the attitude of external agencies, outside the educational system here, and on the continent, towards achieving overall standards of discipline, in and out of school, is most marked. In the writer's experience of schools in France and West Germany, external sanctions and deterrents imposed by parents on pupils alongside community support and approval for teacher-based discipline are an accepted and concomitant part of the total pattern of school-community relationships. Here, apart from a minority of actively supporting parents, and some ambivalent national pressure groups, community attitudes vary, from at the worst, an openly hostile and critical resentment towards a school's attempts to solve what are mainly externally created problems, and at best a benevolent neutrality. This latter often manifests itself in the form of friendly criticisms and suggestions from one group that the school should impose stricter punitive measures and from another that the school should cease imposing any punitive measures. Few, if any, suggestions are offered as to how the community might begin to put its own house in order and so alleviate the school's difficulties.

Having tried to establish the idea that social climate, atmosphere, or tone, call it what you will, have the most telling effect on discipline in general in any school, account has to be taken of the pupil's different status in a middle school's organizational structure. A thirteen-year-old girl for example, is still a thirteen-year-old girl, with all that that implies, whether in a secondary, middle, senior high school, or upper school. In the middle school however, she is, uniquely, and is aware of being, at the top of the school, and her own, her peers', and her teachers' perceptions of her attitudes and behaviour will be adjusted accordingly. Similarly, the faster-growing eleven-year-old boy, who in Shakespearean terms 'bestrides the narrow world' (of his top primary class) 'like a colossus', is a fairly diminutive mid-streamer in a middle school, and the very humblest of small fry in the big pool of the new all-through secondary. Later in this chapter some middle-school teachers give necessarily shortened versions of some actual middle school problems encountered by them, which may serve to reinforce the view that social climate has the force and importance suggested earlier. One additional factor is of relevance when reviewing middle school discipline: the school's social climate will be considerably affected, not simply because of the size and number of age-groups, but by the uniquely awkward range – the range which bridges the gap between childhood and adolescence and which has perhaps been the least studied stage of human development. Least studied perhaps, either because basically less interesting than the more stable groups on either side, or because the unpredictable reactions and spasmodic behaviour patterns of children at this stage are difficult to research.

This age of pre-adolescence, with all its attendant miseries of puberty, was dubbed by an American source in 1946 as 'the period of time, when the nicest children begin behaving in a most awful way'.[2] It is still true that during this time a child, even from the most caring home, could change from a reasonable, adaptable human being into a self-centred, absorbed, moody, sloppy and rude introvert, who drives parents to distraction and will 'try it on' with teachers and other figures of authority. Puberty is the time for an uprising of instinctive drives, previously repressed, and for the painful process of breaking the chains of reliance on parents and seeking approval from the peer group. That teachers find pubescents, as individuals, uncooperative and parents find them annoying may still generally hold good, but there remains to the advantage of middle-school teachers a generally healthy desire to compete, to win approval, individual or group, for academic or athletic performances and a corporate pride in, and sense of identity with, the school. A later American writer on middle school progress in the USA has coined the rather ugly, but apt word 'transescence' to describe this stage of development in children which begins prior to the onset of puberty and extends through the early period of adolescence.[3]

It is not the intention of this chapter to describe middle schools nor to defend their existence – there is indeed no specific line separating childhood from adolescence; nevertheless, if by definition, a middle school covers this 'transescence' period for all its pupils, its social climate and hence its disciplinary policy will be largely influenced by this special factor. Some of the shorter dictionary definitions of discipline appear under the two ascriptions of noun and verb, as follows: 'Noun sub. Subjection to control, order, severe training, mortification, instrument of penance, or punishment. Verb. trans. to *educate*. From the derivative Latin verbs of "educare" – to rear – and "educere" – to lead.' It would seem that the definition of education itself as 'bringing up', teaching, instructing, etc. has a special significance for the implementation of a middle school's disciplinary code during this 'rearing' or 'growing up' period of children's lives. A logical extension from 'bringing up', a well-defined and accepted responsibility for parents, would be 'caring for', even 'cherishing', and hence a moving away from the ferocities of the noun definition, for teachers of the age-range as well as for parents. Between the wars, there was little doubt in the minds of many secondary school teachers, with strong support from parents, about where the emphasis should lie. For those of us secondary-educated during those years, there will be a similar image, vividly called to mind, of the Latin master, whose 'instrument of penance' was the ferula, poised over a petrified pupil struggling with the perplexities of *De Bello*, or the Georgics, with the menacing injunction 'Read or bleed, boy!'

Teaching was then and to some extent still is, at this level, influenced by the Victorian emphasis on strict discipline and the concept of children as miniature adults. They were idle creatures, who needed tough treatment, knowledge was acquired by a process of transferable training, and what was taught was irrelevant so long as they didn't like it. If that might be considered a caricature in these days when modern curricular theorists are at pains to stress the importance of the 'affective' side of children's learning, the remark of the visiting Grammar School Headmaster to the Head of a newly opened middle school may be worth recording – 'All that you seem to be doing here is to keep them happy at their work.'

Most, if not all, secondary schools, will have now either discarded or certainly greatly modified punitive-based codes of conduct which sought to force pupils to conform to a particular pattern of approved control, in favour of a deliberate and reasoned attempt to educate students into wanting self-imposed high standards of behaviour. Such a task, given the instanced characteristics of the pubescent child, may be correspondingly more difficult for the middle-school teachers, but given consistency and continuity of approach to the problem, the goal is attainable, in the form of a social climate founded on mutual respect of teachers by and for their charges.

If, in spite of these efforts, and their acceptance by the majority of pupils, there is continued resistance to them by individuals, then coercive measures will have to be taken and confrontation not evaded. It is when such crucial encounters take place that the discipline, *of the staff*, as an entity, will decide the issue, as one of the following examples illustrates.

Some guidelines culled from experience of service in middle schools and which have helped towards the formation of a working disciplinary policy are given with due diffidence below. They are far from exhaustive, may not necessarily have general applicability and are by no means novel or instant solutions to disciplinary difficulties:

1 Children at this stage react and respond to what we are and what we do, more than to what we say or teach. This is not to belittle in any way a teacher's rightful and passionate concern for the discipline of his or her subject, but the sensitive and intelligent people we have in our schools should recognize that they are primarily there *to enhance the quality of children's lives.*

2 If children recognize and observe your care for them they will be more often prepared to obey your commandments – cf. the biblical injunction 'If you love me keep my commandments.' John 15–16.

3 This caring is a better spur to learning than fear or an aloof and permanently severe posture.

4 Every child should have some experience of success, in however circumscribed a way, and have that success acclaimed and built upon. Even though much time and patience has to be exhausted in the process, the resulting disciplinary improvement is gratifying and contrasts greatly with the lamentable effects of incessant failure on *both parties.*

5 Children need to believe that our concern that they should reach high standards of work achievement, through self-control, is based on this care for them, and for their future interest rather

than on our own, not entirely unreasonable interest as staff, that peace should reign throughout the school, *'per omnia saecula saeculorum'*.

6 An ounce of encouragement, if one may be permitted to use traditional standards of measurements, is worth a ton of disparagement. We should look for things to praise and yet not let anything pass unnoticed that is below our reasonable expectation of a pupil's performance or behaviour.

7 Responsibility should be given not only to those children who are obviously competent to discharge it but to those also who need to exercise it because they are ready for the experience of responsibility. We shall be let down in this respect, and very often, but if a nice judgment is exercised between degree of responsibility demanded, and pupil's capacity to perform it, persistence will pay due rewards.

8 Self-control, and responsibility, on the part of the children comes from deliberate attempts by staff to inspire confidence, to cultivate initiative and sensitivity. The more staff are aware of the different kinds of pressure, good and bad, to which children are subject, and especially of the ways in which individuals are specifically handicapped the greater will be their capacity to counteract the harmful influences and build on the helpful ones.

9 Accentuate the positive, including positive good manners. This gives teachers more room for manoeuvre. Would-be awkward and defiant pubescents get less opportunity to score a series of victories against demands *not* to do certain things, and so bring damaging confrontations with head-on collisions of will and determination.

For inexperienced teachers whose discipline is precarious, such situations bring havoc in their train.

10 If the price of liberty is eternal vigilance, then staff can gradually relax formal demands for duty supervision, by exercising constant vigilance in a corporate sense, and being vigilant as individuals in keeping standards of self-discipline.

This is not simply care in observing professional integrity in terms of punctuality, work-preparation, and consideration for colleagues, but in having consideration for, and also displaying good manners towards, children.

Finally, before setting down one or two accounts, without further comment, of particular teachers' handling of situations which arose, there is one priceless asset which if teachers are not born with they must certainly cultivate – a sense of humour. It is essential that no middle school lacks teachers capable of both exuding a sense of fun and gaiety and of laughing at themselves. If a soft answer turns away wrath, nothing defuses an explosive situation more readily sometimes than the apposite comical remark which points up its absurd side.

Children of this age relish comedy situations and love telling jokes to the point of utter tedium for the teacher, whose sense of humour will be somewhat more sophisticated: but this childish sense of humour can be made capital of when the occasion arises, for example to make analogies with the 'absurdity' of their own behaviour.

An example of a problem of discipline
(twelve-year-old girl – male teacher)

The problem
Having been with a new class for only four days I walked into the class-room after dinner time. The full class were waiting. One boy at once addressed me gleefully, 'Don't look at the board, sir!' Scrawled there was a very uncomplimentary comment about a girl in the class, a four-letter word, and the signature Jennifer. Jennifer was not in the room.

My reaction
I rubbed the words out quietly and enquired where Jennifer was. The same boy was quick to answer that she had gone out and he thought she had run off. Clearly confrontation and disapproval, heavily applied, were inappropriate. Firstly, because it was suspicious that the message was signed and that information was so forthcoming. It was possible that someone else was responsible. Secondly, if the signature was correct, this particular girl was well known for outrageous outbursts. From all that I knew of her she seemed to fear rejection above all and, so soon in our relationship, I could not risk confrontation even if that was what she was after. Thirdly, even without this consideration, confrontation is a difficult thing to manage to the teacher's advantage, it is against my style of discipline and it was too soon in the year to risk it.

I made no comment about the words on the board since it was obvious that I disapproved strongly. I disliked the way in which the boy was enjoying getting Jennifer into trouble and it was this point I made very forcibly to him. It had to be said and, for a moment, it changed the focus of the situation. I then went to look for Jennifer.

She was outside putting something into her locker. She was apparently neither upset nor very defensive. When I asked if she had written some-thing on the board she confessed to the phrase about the girl but denied the swear word. I made it clear that I disapproved and that other ways should be found to express one's feelings. I knew she was an accomplished liar but chose not to disbelieve her this time. We went back into the classroom together. No further comment was made about the incident.

Follow up
It was clear that Jennifer was waiting to see if I would reject her. It was

also clear that Jennifer and a group of boys were feuding (other things such as fighting and name-calling confirmed this). The next time a feuding incident occurred I took the boys and Jennifer aside separately and told them I did not want their argument to spill over into the classroom. I would not listen to either party's justifications. I hoped thereby to be able, on future occasions not to stand on either side and yet to show at the same time that this behaviour was unacceptable. Until I was clearer about what was going on between them I needed to avoid coming to any hard conclusions.

Another example of a problem of discipline
(the same twelve-year-old girl – female teacher)

Jennifer is not in my class, nor do I know her particularly well, as it was her first history lesson with me. However, her reputation had gone before her, and it was no real surprise when she started playing up immediately.

She was in a bad mood when she came into the classroom. (I learned later that she had already been in trouble that afternoon with a senior member of staff for defending a younger brother or sister in the first year.) I had already divided the children into three groups for history projects, and had a limited number of books available from the Teachers' library. In addition, I had prepared three worksheets, each containing about fifteen suggestions for areas of study, all related to the contents of the books. I asked the class to look at the books, then at the worksheets, then to come to me when their choice of an area of study had been made, when I would write their names on the sheet next to the task chosen. Meanwhile, I circulated among the groups, making suggestions, pointing out interesting pictures in the books, etc. During this time Mary expressed a wish to study Edwardian wedding trousseaux. I agreed and went to put her name on the list. However, Jennifer's name was already there. Quite amicably I pointed out that Mary had already asked me, that she had followed the proper procedure, and I asked Jennifer to make another choice. (I knew that there was only one book with suitable material in it, and that this would already be in use by another girl before Mary got her turn.) Jennifer's reaction was immediate. 'Reight then, if I can't do wedding trousseaux I'm doing nowt.' I tried humouring her, pointing out interesting alternatives, but she wasn't to be diverted. She kept treating me to very aggrieved, baleful stares, followed by unnecessarily loud 'Hurry up with that book. I'm having it next, not her' ('her' being Mary). I considered having a major confrontation, but it seemed unwise in her first lesson when I knew so little about her, and she wasn't actually stopping the others from working, so I let her continue. At one point she left the classroom, shouting that she was 'off to the library to find summat on wedding trousseaux'. I followed her, took hold of her arm, saying, 'You don't leave the classroom without my permission', led her back to her place, then left her alone. At the end of the lesson she had done no work, and was still muttering 'I writ my name on that list first; I'm doing it, not her.'

I discussed the situation with her class teacher and her class teacher of the previous year and thought about it during the evening. I was determined not to give in to her. However, I didn't want her to waste another lesson, and though it was possible she would have forgotten about it by next week, it didn't seem likely – she was so determined to have her own way. I felt there had to be compromise if we were to achieve a working relationship for the rest of the year. I therefore asked her class teacher to excuse her for the last lesson on Friday, and asked Miss Cooper if she would like to do some work with Jennifer then. Next I sent for Jennifer. She was highly suspicious, but not hostile. She agreed that she would like to do the work on Friday, and seemed to accept it when I said, 'but of course you won't be able to use the book next Thursday afternoon'. It remains to be seen whether she will choose something else from the list. If she refuses I shall set her some French. Mary is having the book during history lessons, and I won't back down on that. Incidentally, Shirley said that Jennifer enjoyed the extra history lesson and worked hard.

There were a number of considerations in my dealing with the situation. Firstly it was my first lesson with this group and I was concerned to appear fair to everyone, (including Mary), and to establish that if I asked for a certain procedure to be followed, then it must be so. However, I also wanted to establish a happy working atmosphere for the rest of the term's work, and if I had taken too strong a line, then that would have been impossible in Jennifer's case. In general I don't believe in side-stepping when a child is spoiling for a confrontation. I feel that ultimately the child senses the teacher's inability to cope and becomes increasingly disruptive, with the result that the eventual confrontation is worse than an earlier one would have been. Nevertheless in this case I think I was right to play for time, partly because I didn't know her well and so could easily have misjudged the amount of force to use, and also because she was already upset, and as a general rule I don't like to deal with a child who is already upset. I feel they need a period of grace in which to lick their wounds. *Two* rejections in an afternoon is too much for a problem child or a sensitive child, though it may be justified in the case of a very confident child.

Notes

1 FINLAYSON, BANKS, LOUGHRAN (1970) NSER University of Liverpool
2 HAVIGHURST, R. J., ROBINSON, M. Z. and DORR, M. (1946) *Journal of Educational Research*
3 EICHORN, D. H. (1966) *The Middle School* New York Library of Education

5 A small and peaceful country town

Geoffrey Goodall
Principal, Lord Williams's School, Thame

Each comprehensive school surely reflects the habits and attitudes of the community it encompasses. Where there are urban problems, the town secondary school is bound to inherit them. If theft or vandalism or racial antagonisms are rife in a town, the local school is hardly likely to escape these ravages. Nor do I think the school has a hope in a hundred of solving such problems single-handed, if in the short run they are soluble at all.

Lord Williams's School is fortunate because it draws its pupils from the small and peaceful country town of Thame, where civic violence is unknown, few wives or children get battered in the home, poverty and bad housing are non-existent, while drunkenness and unemployment are rare. Perhaps for these reasons, if for no other, the school has not yet seen a pupil assault a teacher.

However, like any other school, it is not without its troublemakers. With over two thousand pupils in the school, which spans the whole of the local community, such a situation is inevitable. We have our share of the local football club's hooligans and a goodly supply of rejected children, aggressive children, neurotic children and maladjusted children. A few have already been through the courts for criminal offences and others are well on the way. Some will be in jail before they are twenty-one. How could it be otherwise when we take the lot, unless of course sin had miraculously disappeared from the world? However, the hard core of almost unbiddable pupils is only a tiny fraction of the whole, possibly about 3 per cent but in a school of two thousand that still adds up to sixty very difficult pupils, twenty of whom are fifteen plus and fairly hefty, just waiting for the day when they can leave and playing merry havoc until that day arrives.

Then we have a second group, those perfectly normal pupils who enjoy a bit of mischief, a laugh at the teacher's expense, or an amusing challenge, especially where they detect weakness. They will misbehave in class but are not hellbent on wrecking the lesson, the teacher or their own education. These pupils are, of course, much more numerous but they are straightforward and one can usually win them round. It is the explosive 3 per cent who really sap our energies and test our ingenuity. One of my main concerns is that they should be prevented from depressing the morale of the staff, damaging the education of those pupils who do wish to learn and destroying the fabric of the school.

There is a third group of pupils who err in the eyes of the school by failing to comply with the prevailing rules. They transgress from time to time by not wearing the school uniform, or by arriving late. They may break bounds or light a fag, they go on talking when silence has been called. They may do these things on principle, they may do them expressly to defy, they may do so out of habit or purely from feebleness and slackness. Beyond the confines of the school, however, some of their offences are not seen in this light. After all, adults elsewhere may smoke and not wear uniform. Within the institution, however, these acts make up a breach of discipline and call for action.

How do we begin to deal with these many varied kinds of indiscipline? How do we cope with the differing thresholds of conformity and cooperative behaviour that each individual child is capable of?

May I say at once that there are a few pupils whom we cannot seem to reform. We fail completely, though not for want of trying, and they leave school with little to show for their last two years except a trail of débris both literal and metaphorical, and sighs of relief from the staff and other pupils. But how do we contain them in the meantime? We try to ensure first that the majority of the pupils do not join them. Because the number of really difficult pupils is small, they can be hived off for senior staff or specially trained staff to cope with. Certainly we do not expect hard-worked young teachers to have to deal with skilled disrupters at the same time as trying to teach the rest of the class. So we operate a limited withdrawal system which isolates the most unmanageable pupils from the mainstream of pupils and staff. Help from other agencies is invaluable here. The school itself has neither the resources nor the expertise to attempt the long and daunting task of cure, reform or rehabilitation of the most anti-social pupils, so we lean heavily on the Educational or Clinical Psychologist, the Welfare Officer, the Probation Officer and the Social Worker, and although their success rate may be small, at least they are specialists, able to view each case in its full context, treat the whole family and use individual expedients.

But how do we keep the 'normal majority' happily on the straight and narrow? For a start we try not to antagonize them gratuitously by having a lot of square pegs in round holes as far as their subjects are concerned. By the time pupils have been with us for three years we have a shrewd idea of their talents and tastes and for their last two years of compulsory school we try to match them to courses which really suit them and which they have freely chosen. For many this may mean a high vocational element, a strong practical bias, extensive bouts of work experience and not a lot of academic study. Among the best aids to discipline in Lord Williams's School are the wood and metalworkshops, where some of our toughest customers are motivated, manageable and busy. It is not just a matter of pacifying fractious youths with a diet of ice-cream and popcorn, for the skills they are learning seem to them to be connected with their long-term career interests and the tasks they are called upon to do are well within their capacity. Similarly the laziest, sulkiest and most negative girls usually become sweetness and light on the 'parentcraft' course. Girls who spit at colleagues, give black eyes to rivals in the loo and incline to truant when the mood takes them, become keen and cooperative when being taught how to manage a toddler and grow more positive still when actual toddlers arrive to be cared for. Would that a few of our boys would opt for this course as well, but they never do. We have no record of misbehaviour or exclusion during parentcraft or metalwork classes and yet the courses cater for some pupils who make other teachers' hair stand on end. Commerce is another example. In the last seven years, no pupil has been detained for bad conduct during typewriting lessons and few have truanted. Nor, so far as I can tell, has a typewriter ever been vandalized, yet we have fifty-four typing lessons a week, attended by some of our most intractable characters. The reason for this success is not hard to find; although these lessons may not altogether teach what offices require later, (in fact they would prefer accurate spelling, punctuation and English grammar) – and although a four-week crash course could achieve just as much as two years of lessons, the pupils themselves *believe* the typewriting to be useful and relevant to them in the world at large. It is also hugely therapeutic. Banging the keys rhythmically is as soothing to some pupils as stirring the glue in the workshop is to others. We need to find more such activities.

These practical subjects appear to the pupils to relate to the adult world of work, but clearly the requirement to earn a living is not the only one of a child's needs that the school must attend to. The school needs to cater for such obvious ones as the need to be able to communicate, to be a decent citizen, to understand one's own body and to cope with domestic family life – from mending a fuse to living in tolerable harmony with one's spouse. We try to foster this all important health education and moral education through several channels. Assemblies and daily form periods are one. RE lessons are another. English and drama with their opportunities for rôle play are another. The Oxford Moral Education Project's 'sensitivity' booklets provide excellent material for getting adolescents to develop self-awareness and an awareness of others. Nor are these the only ways in which pupils may strengthen their skill at interpersonal relations. Surely the most potent area of all for educating the emotions is that of the arts. That is why we build music, dance, drama and art quite substantially into the curriculum, and into extensive extra-mural activities. We believe that young human beings have strong imaginations and emotions whose powerful needs we ignore at our peril.

Some indiscipline stems not from pent-up emotions but from pent-up physical energies and so these too need considerable outlets. The most obvious one for these surplus energies is a vigorous and diverse sports programme, with plenty of 'outward bound' activities thrown in. Clearly not all pupils need the challenge of rugby or swimming, nor should they always have to participate, but most do enjoy them and find in the training, the tensions, the struggles and the results, a measure of fulfilment. Furthermore, to do any sport well involves a high degree of self-discipline as well as the more obvious collective discipline. So both the arts and games offer pupils countless small opportunities for leadership, responsibility and for cooperative ventures, which demand a great deal of

broad curriculum, therefore, plus a hefty
'ivities, finely tuned to differing individuals,
criptions for ensuring reasonable discipline

ssive proviso: the actual teaching of each
and appetizing and this competence will
he individual teacher. The wish of nearly
od' teachers and they get very resentful if
off with poor teachers. What is more, the
and only rarely have I ever come across
as a 'good' teacher having been given a

Important qualities in my view are: charis... ier steel, clarity, the possession of clearly visible pe... te a bit of acting skill and a sense of humour. On the issue of classroom discipline, most of these qualities are real assets. Obviously the teacher needs to be likeable or the pupils are unlikely to be responsive. However, there is a world of difference between having warmth and simply seeking popularity. Few pupils respect the teacher who is a pushover any more than the one who is a tyrant.

Likewise an awareness of what the pupils are thinking and feeling – seeing the world through their eyes, will help the sensitive teacher to temper his lessons accordingly.

Being clear and definite is not only important when explaining new material. Children expect their teachers to know exactly what to do next. If a teacher does not take charge of the situation, the class will do it for him. This is where careful planning and training is so vital, even down to the minutiae of marking a register in time for the class to reach assembly.

Then again, pupils expect teachers to be teachers and not like one of their mates. This includes the teacher's language, his appearance and his behaviour. No class will thank him for being scruffy, speaking shoddily, arriving late, allowing mayhem or being offensive to them.

One of the key things for a young teacher in managing a class is to be fair yet firm. Experience is the best guide here, but one thing is certain, it does not do to utter threats which one may not be able to implement. If the teacher says, for example: 'I will punish the next person who talks', he may find he cannot identify the next culprit and then he is landed with burdensome, unpopular and possibly ineffectual sleuth work. Or the next person to talk may do so by accident, or may be the best behaved pupil in the class, or there may be confusion. The trouble with seeking a culprit is that it begins to resemble a hunt, and so the whole class may take up that game. Above all, he will try to avoid punishing the whole class for bad behaviour which he cannot track down to one individual or where only half the class is responsible. Nor is shouting at a noisy class very often effective. Pupils who think that they are being insensitively treated soon become resentful and respond in a similar way. Gerald Haigh says in *The Reluctant Adolescent*: 'In this direction lies unbridled chaos with the would-be figure of authority screaming ineffective orders at an openly defiant class.' Happily, very few pupils are out to destroy their teachers and most are motivated by fun rather than malice.

The greatest single aid to ensuring good classroom control, is for the teacher to build up strong relationships with his pupils over a period of time. I don't begin to teach any French to my first-year classes until I know a little about each pupil personally. Pressing on with the syllabus is secondary. As Haigh says:

> The building up of a relationship will take a very long time, during which there is a great deal of unspoken bargaining about boundaries which surround acceptable classroom behaviour. Eventually, after much patience, the boundaries will be fixed and the pupils will observe them without too much fuss. A teacher who has been with a class for a long time and who has an apparently easy and relaxed relationship with them, may well give the impression of having a very cushy job, but this ease and relaxation has been hard won by the constant use of professional skill and judgment. One of the easiest mistakes for a young teacher to make is to leap in and emulate the surface characteristics of an experienced teacher without taking account of the need to spend months in building up the ground rules. The experienced teacher's classroom is relaxed and calm because the class have tried all the dodges already and failed. The new teacher cannot in any way short circuit the system and plug into it beyond the testing stage. Nor must he misunderstand this and think himself a failure because he cannot manage a class with the apparent ease of his seniors. Adolescents will not be bullied into working and permanent confrontation is as destructive in a school as it is in the world at large. The real crux of the matter lies in the personality of the teacher. Adolescents will cooperate with a teacher whom they respect, almost regardless of the content of his lesson and they will play havoc with a teacher they despise, even though his lessons are full of lively 'relevance'.

One thing the skilled teacher will always seek to do, and that is to build up the confidence and self-esteem of his pupils. This occurs most readily where there is plenty of praise and encouragement in class – but first there has to be something meriting praise and it is here that the teacher's skill is most needed. He has constantly to engineer little advances, small areas of success for even the least talented pupils and this calls for immense skill in matching the level of difficulty to the individual's thresholds of understanding, in motivating him to keep going, if need be lending him some of one's own enthusiasm, and in presenting the work in such a step-like way that every pupil can make the transitions, however small.

There is a third factor in this business of overall discipline. The quality of a school's resources and of its environment cannot fail to matter. A good level of corporate discipline must surely be more readily attainable in a boarding school than in a day school, more attainable in schools with spacious recreation areas, fields and trees than in high-rise boxes wedged between factories and council estates.

Of course, all the fine surroundings and splendid equipment will be of no avail unless the overriding ethos of the school is right. The ideal, it seems to me, is where a basically sympathetic atmosphere prevails but is backed by 'benevolent rigour'. Sloppy, weak and ineffectual staff are just as damaging for youngsters as hostile and sarcastic ones. The school should be organized so that a clear framework of support and responsibilities (for both pupils and staff) is visible to all. Provision must be there to meet the moments of crisis and trouble which pupils or indeed teachers undergo and this pattern should enable experienced teachers to assist and guide their younger colleagues as well as to cope with the more dramatic cases of disorder.

Such things as the school rules can create discipline problems. If there are too few rules, the bully boys hold sway and their values predominate; if there are too many rules, the school is simply creating more felons and making a rod for its own back. The rules that do obtain need to be self-evidently reasonable and ones which most of the pupils and not just the staff and parents can readily accept. We on the staff deplore swearing at Lord Williams's School but swearing is part of the normal home life of a number of pupils and they see nothing wrong in it. So whilst a teacher needs to stop it if he hears it, he would be wise not to overreact or to regard the event as a heinous offence. However, if a respected teacher makes it repeatedly clear that he objects to swearing, it is likely that inveterate swearers will not swear in his presence, that is unless they expressly wish to wound or to confront him, and then the problem is a bigger one than merely swearing – it is one of maladjustment and calls for major measures.

It also helps if there is some sort of pupil body which can get rules removed, altered or added, thus giving pupils some say in rule-making and some control, however small, over the rules under which they operate. I believe it is a good thing for a school and good training for pupils that they should be involved in rule enforcement, in supervision, in monitoring and in duties of various kinds, although I am not sure how far pupils should impose sanctions.

Then there are the less formal aspects of institutional life. The way teachers are seen to treat parents, or treat each other, the way they treat pupils, the way senior pupils treat each other, and the way they treat the younger ones in their charge – all these things create a tide and a tone which provides a powerful example and will most certainly have an effect on the discipline of the pupils within the school. Newcomers will readily adapt to the prevailing current. But how do you establish one in the first place? The head and his staff have to will it and then to will the means. This calls for the staff to be consistent and rigorous as a body, and it also means carrying with you the senior pupils, whose example counts for so much. Finally it means establishing a careful routine and a set of habits. Then there is some chance that good order will be the norm.

Alas, some pupils misbehave however they are handled and Lord Williams's School has the usual set of sanctions. These range from the traditional ticking off by various hierarchs to suspension from school. On the way they include: letters which inform parents of a pupil's misdemeanours, impositions, public works, removal of privileges or advancement, lunch time or Saturday detentions, exclusion from certain classes, even the use of the cane on certain rare occasions, and visits from members of outside agencies – from educational psychologists to local policemen and finally the bringing-in of parents. Two of the most potent consequences of bad behaviour are when a pupil's self-image is damaged or when he knows that he has upset those he loves and who love him. Sadly, some of the worst delinquents know no such love and this is obviously why they behave as they do. With all our sanctions, we try to be fair, to take trouble, and to preserve some sort of relationship with the pupil. We do not think that we can root out sin either by sanctions or by more positive means, so that the school's measures are sometimes little more than palliatives. My view is that home values, street values and peer-group values generally count for more with a pupil than those values which a school may unilaterally seek to impart, but that is no reason for a school not to try. Take for example, the offence of stealing. Although stealing is probably ineradicable, we try to persuade all pupils that theft is wrong and harmful. But at the same time one must also provide robust lockable lockers, supervise cloakrooms, warn pupils not to bring valuables or at least to hand them in; where necessary we conduct searches, punish offenders and ensure subsequent treatment. Though all these measures divert our energies momentarily from teaching and may even introduce an atmosphere of suspicion, they do at least keep the number of thefts in check; there are no easy pickings for thieves and we have demonstrated that we care about it.

This is our policy with other offences too. It can be very wearing. Indeed, one of the least pleasant aspects of being a hierarch is that one runs the risk of being a Lord High Punisher, spending an inordinate amount of time chastising miscreants who have caused trouble. It can be particularly difficult because the head of a large school cannot know all the pupils and therefore has to dispense sanctions, as it were, in a vacuum and without any positive relationship with the offender to offset the sanction. But a head, if he is wise, will still do these thing to provide a structure of support for the staff. He will not stand by and watch the morale of a good teacher or even a good class being steadily eroded by seasoned campaigners. They are to my mind best extracted from the class.

One last word, which I give to people who ask me what sort of punishment is most effective for a disruptive pupil, as if any punishment could ever do the trick by itself: if you love a child and that child knows that you care, it doesn't really matter, within reason, what sanctions you choose, and this may include corporal punishment. If on the other hand, you dislike a child and that child knows you do not value him, then whatever sanctions you use will be doomed, indeed if you omit to punish altogether, you are still doomed because what really matters in the last resort, is not the force of the retribution you administer but the force of the bond between you.

6   The Creighton experience

Molly Hattersley
Headmistress, Creighton School, London

I watched one of the opening games of the 1978–9 football league season in a Lancashire town with a proud tradition of achievement in the game. Loyalties might have been expected to run high since both the home team and their opponents are used to playing in the first division and have not taken kindly to their comparatively recent descent into the second. Independent Television Sport were filming for *The Big Match* programme on the following day. The stand opposite the one in which we were sitting had been vertically divided into three sections. On the left, the supporters of the home team, on the right, the supporters of the visiting team, and in the middle, a number of policemen and their dogs. Throughout the match, the rival supporters, massed against the iron railings which prevented them from entering 'no man's land', devoted much of their attention to each other and hardly any to the football. They uttered well-rehearsed threats in perfect unison, sang versions of well-known songs in fair tune and time and shook their fists as one at the opposing faction. Their ages ranged from about twelve to seventeen. Most of them spend their weekdays in school.

The schools which they attend do not exist in a vacuum; they are part of contemporary society, and are the product of its values and needs, not their creator. Over the last twenty years the reorganization of secondary education, itself the result of a rethinking of values, has been only one of many quite considerable changes in social institutions and attitudes. Enormous scientific and technological advance, increased prosperity, greater social mobility, movements for reform in the laws which provide the framework of discipline for society as a whole, a decline in religious belief, the huge and underrated influence of television, have directly affected the *mores* of our basic social unit, the family. Children now grow and develop in a society which is itself less strictly 'disciplined' in the traditional sense than ever before.

Although the relaxation of attitudes is in general to be welcomed because of the greater freedom of thought and action it offers, the problems it raises are considerable, not least for the schools. They have the responsibility of providing for all their pupils the opportunity to develop their talents and capabilities to the full. They must ensure that the atmosphere in which the pupils work will enable them to do this. But schools cannot separate and insulate themselves from the climate and atmosphere of the society of which they are an integral part. They are undoubtedly accountable to that society, but that society is responsible for them.

Anxieties about standards are an inevitable corollary to change. It is hardly surprising that such anxieties should focus particularly on schools, on which society's hopes for the future rest. The dilemma for those responsible for the creation and maintenance of standards in schools today, especially standards of behaviour, is this: should the school seek to counteract the influences in society which have resulted in a relaxation of traditional discipline, or should the school's expectations and attitudes in the matter take account of and accommodate such influences? Most schools attempt a compromise, a balance between the two. Getting the balance right is extremely difficult and absolutely essential. To take too little account of influences in the world outside school and make demands which either cannot be met or cannot be justified will set up destructive conflicts and hostilities, which will certainly interfere with the school's work. To demand too little is a recipe for under-achievement of all kinds at best, and anarchy at worst. Every school has to decide positively about this matter: decide on its aims and philosophy, make its arrangements accordingly and ensure that they are followed.

My own school days were spent in régimes which were rigidly disciplined, and hindsight does not lead me to regret the gradual change which has led to a decline in deference and an increase in questioning. Relationships based on mutual respect are more difficult to achieve than those based on fear but infinitely more valuable to both teacher and child. To ask even awkward questions is to display that intellectual curiosity which schools should nurture. But there can be no doubt that the tasks imposed on schools in today's society are infinitely more complex and onerous than was the case in a less enlightened but more certain age, and this is particularly so in matters of behaviour. A school staff must undertake by means of discussion and agreement about common aims to establish a framework of order which is generally understood and accepted as being in the interests of all, with enough flexibility to allow for the development of relationships and enough strength to withstand the testing which it will inevitably receive.

For comprehensive schools, in particular, the problems of satisfying every level of public expectation are acute. Much of the generalized criticism which one hears about standards of discipline and of academic performance are judgments made on partial evidence, some of it certainly adduced to support a call for a return to the selective system. The comprehensive school must be prepared to live with opinion of this sort, however ill-informed.

It may be worth considering why such schools are so vulnerable, and why they have to take particular care to ensure that even though prejudiced opinion is unlikely to move in their favour, there is no justification for any general feeling that they are failing to provide a properly organized framework in which learning of all kinds can take place. In a selective school the attitudes of staff, parents and children are likely to be conditioned to some extent by the judgments which have already been made about the special abilities of the children who have been admitted. Of course those children are subject to the influence of contemporary society as are all others but in that they have been deemed to be in a special and desirable category, they must regard themselves as different. They and their parents will be anxious to justify that judgment in their response to the school's standards of work and behaviour. Children from the least advantaged section of society are unlikely to have qualified for entry: those who have done so are clearly not suffering the major handicap of limited intelligence.

The comprehensive school, on the other hand, is a microcosm of society as a whole, gladly accepting children of all abilities and backgrounds, and regarding the education of each of them as being of equal value. The school must be aware of all the problems and all the pressures which can affect the progress and welfare of this varied community and the conditions which may affect the behaviour of their boys and girls when they are not at school. Even in the most supportive families quite heavy responsibilities may be placed upon the children. The routine of daily life for many urban children will involve their leaving home after both parents have gone to work and leaving school long before either parent can be at home. A growing number of children (13 per cent on the evidence published in 1976 by the National Children's Bureau) are not living with both natural parents. Children belonging to minority ethnic groups, however affluent and well-housed their families may be, and many of them are not, have to face the strains which constantly restoked controversy imposes on them.

Schools and parents have to compete for the attention of young people with the determined onslaught made on them by pop culture, television and by commercial interests of all kinds. An alternative conformity is offered which is immediately attractive. Some young people who adopt it do not find it easy to subdue, when they are in school.

Within the school, the do's and don'ts of everyday life must take into account the fact that pupils vary in age from young children to young adults, and in ability from those whose understanding is immediate to those for whom patient and frequent explanation is essential.

Many comprehensive schools, Creighton among them, have to work in buildings which were not designed for the purpose. The problems produced by split sites, with scattered laboratories, workshops, drama halls, gymnasia, and the additional and extensive movement which they involve, increase the complexity of arrangements which have to be understood by all. At Creighton, for example, the design of the larger of the two main buildings makes it impossible for the children to move across the four-storey building except at ground level. The difficulties created by such physical limitations are directly relevant to the behaviour of the children. Concentration, time, books, tempers, all may be lost as you hurry, or not, between one teaching area and another. The atmosphere of the school is obviously affected by these extraneous factors. The influence which can be brought to bear by emphasizing care for and appreciation of one's immediate environment is more difficult to achieve in such circumstances.

The task of creating the sort of atmosphere which will be conducive to the school's aims must be undertaken with all these factors in mind. The 'discipline', the atmosphere, and the attitudes of the comprehensive school are inevitably part of that 'hidden curriculum', recently discussed by Her Majesty's Inspectors (Curricula 11–16) as 'the approved procedures and forms of conduct through which the school conveys implicit values'. The values thus conveyed will depend not only on what the child is told, or told to do, but on what he sees going on around him, on what he takes in day by day, often unconsciously, about the standards which are valued in the school, and on the environment in which he has to work.

The nature of discipline in these terms is misunderstood by many who would like to see a greater emphasis on what they think it is. In their terms, it has a great deal to do with punishment and coercion. 'Discipline' is something which is applied to those whose behaviour offends. The implication of this limited view is that good behaviour is dependent on compulsion and threat. But, although coercion is obviously necessary for a minority, most schools prefer to work on the assumption that children will behave reasonably if they know what is expected of them. Schools see it as an essential duty to make clear to their pupils not only what is expected but why. In a well-ordered school the stress must always be on the positive value to be gained from behaving in a controlled and considerate fashion within the framework which the school has laid down.

The success of a positive and constructive approach of this kind will depend on the quality, strength and unity of the staff. Every teacher in the school is involved in some way through his responsibilities within the pastoral system, in caring for the personal development of individual children. Every teacher has a responsibility both in his teaching and elsewhere in the school for maintaining an atmosphere which enables the school to work productively, which gives the children a sense of stability and confidence and at the same time teaches them the value of order. And every teacher has a vested interest in the success of these arrangements, for without them he is unable to work effectively.

The general organization of the school must strengthen his ability to provide the guidance and advice which children expect from him. His personal control will inevitably be tested from time to time, sometimes in conditions of extreme difficulty. Lines of communication must be very clear so that the teacher not only knows where to find support if he needs it, but knows also that such support is an accepted part of the school's arrangements. Teachers must be able to have confidence that those who endanger the fabric of the school's life will not be allowed to destroy it. The gulf between the behaviour patterns of the majority of children, testing though these can sometimes be, and the extremes of violence and rejection which can be exhibited by a tiny minority, is one of the greatest difficulties faced by both the individual teacher and the school staff as a whole in finding a balance which will meet the interests of all. The confidence of teachers and children in the code of behaviour adopted by the school is crucial. The head of the school must constantly take its temperature and prescribe if necessary.

A key factor in that condition of working together which builds a community is the extent to which children feel committed to it. If pupils are involved in activities which go on outside the classroom, to which they can choose to give their time, energy and enthusiasm, in drama, music, sport, and social service of all kinds, this will not only widen their horizons and increase their enjoyment, but will also greatly influence their response to the demands which the school makes on them.

Inevitably, any system designed to ensure that the community can work without unnecessary restraints but in an orderly and productive manner, must include sanctions of some kinds. The minority, and it always is a minority, whose actions interfere with the agreed order of things, must be dealt with if the interests of the majority are to be defended. Methods which are both constructive and instructive can be devised for those whose offences are the usual and perhaps inevitable attempt of the young to 'get round' the constraints imposed upon them by their elders. The system is bound to be tested in this way, and it must respond. Thus, those who do not do the work cheerfully done by others will find such tasks even more time consuming than if they had responded in the first place. Those who find it difficult to be punctual will find their day lengthened as a result. Those who make the place untidy or ugly will spend some of their own time putting matters right. Those whose enjoyment of their friends' company interferes not only with their own concentration but that of others will find themselves temporarily removed from temptation. Those who show that they need daily monitoring of work and behaviour will receive it. The checks and balances which rightly and inevitably curtail individual freedom in the interests of a free and civilized society must be the same in school as elsewhere. And an understanding of the need for those checks and balances should be part of every child's education. For most children, these constraints, imposed in the name of the general good will suffice. They will not in all cases be accepted without question, but an important lesson will be learned by many of those involved, even if the process is a lengthy one.

There will, however, be a number of children, a small but significant number, with severe behavioural difficulties, whose attitudes and conduct towards other children, teachers and the community in general take little account of generally accepted patterns. Clearly such children impose enormous strains on the system and everybody in it. They are almost certainly in need of skilled help of the kind the school is not equipped to give. The school's attempts to arrange for such help are often frustrated. To say that the school itself must provide what help it can is self-evident but this means that in some cases an intractable problem is being wrestled with. If the staff react to anti-social behaviour within the school's normal framework by imposing sanctions of the kind outlined above, what are they to do with a boy or girl whose behaviour is persistently and some-times violently disruptive and uncontrolled? The severity of any punishment the school is likely to be willing or able to impose is limited and in any case a severely punitive reaction merely confirms the child's feeling of rejection and may strengthen the attitudes which motivate his disruptive behaviour. (Those who imagine that corporal punishment is the answer might examine the punishment books of schools where it is commonly used, where they are likely to find the same names recurring with depressing regularity.)

The only way to attempt to meet the twin problems of helping the child to come to terms with the school community and defending the interests of all its other members is to use all the strengths of the pastoral system. The staff involved must have time to give the individual coun-selling and guidance that are needed, to begin to build a relationship in which mutual trust can develop, to involve parents, and to call upon those outside the school whose expertise and experience may be vital. Consistent support of this kind can sometimes enable a damaged child to learn to live reasonably in a community which is demonstrating its anxiety not to reject him. Often, however, the damage done by years of neglect, over-indulgence, deprivation and the many other disadvantages which a proportion of our children have to suffer, is so great that no ordinary school can succeed in bringing about any improvement. The amount of time and effort spent on trying to do so inevitably endangers and sometimes destroys the balance which is so necessary for the health of the whole community.

This is why even the most caring staffs, even the most experienced teachers, are seeking to have the needs of this small minority of children dealt with on a more individual basis than is possible in the long term in an ordinary school. Various ways of doing this are now being tried, some of them involving special arrangements and additional support within the normal school, some attempting to help such children in small self-contained groups where teaching and therapy can go on at the same time, others combining some attendance at school with alternative provision elsewhere. More of these schemes are needed. In a comprehensive school of 1,000, if only 1 per cent are in this category, the school will have ten pupils, each needing special, continuous and individual help. The setting up of special units, centres and sanctuaries will not solve the problem, which has its roots in a variety of ills outside the schools, but such ar-rangements are a positive attempt to meet a special need. The alternative in the most extreme cases is the child's total rejection by his school in the form of suspension, the last straw for him and the school, and usually the culmination of a long process of failure on both sides. Years of experience, often involving lack of success in dealing with this sort of child, have convinced me of the need for the closest liaison between those responsible in school and those perhaps even more responsible outside it: social workers, probation officers, education welfare officers, magistrates, doctors, psychologists, therapists, the police – and above all parents. Comprehensive schools deal with children whose parents have themselves suffered these same limitations and deprivations. Our society, which has widened the horizons of so many children, must find better ways of helping those whose hope of moving successfully from childhood into adulthood is blighted and who are unable to grasp with growing maturity the opportunities which will enable them to live happy and fulfilled lives as citizens and as parents. While the continuous cycle of deprivation goes on, schools must try to cope with the casualties, but they often fail.

At Creighton, working in the context of all the factors I have described, the staff are trying to create an atmosphere for living and learning which will enable our children to grow as individuals, as members of a community and as future members of society. Arrangements governing behaviour in the school are the result of extensive staff discussion and are intended to encourage the development of self-discipline, but the essential sanctions are there for the protection of the majority and to support teachers of widely varying experience. We depend greatly for the success of these arrangements on the support of parents, all of whom have the opportunity, even before their children enter the school, to learn something of its atmosphere and attitudes through meetings held both before and after the choice of school is made. Thereafter strong contact is maintained with parents by means of the usual structure of reports, parents' evenings, interviews etc. and through the activities of the Creighton Association. Those whose children are having difficulties themselves or providing them for others rarely fail to come and discuss the problem with us and almost invariably support the staff in their attempts to find a solution.

Our system is not entirely successful: the balance we are seeking is delicate and it does not always maintain its equilibrium. Not all children can easily respond to the demands which it makes on their capacity for self-control and self-discipline: not all staff are in tune with its theory or its practice and some of those who are have their confidence shaken from time to time. But on the whole it works for us. The influence of a 'hidden curriculum' on the development of individual children cannot be seen from one day to another; it cannot be accurately assessed at all. Hunter Davies ended his portrait of a year in the life of Creighton School by expressing this view:

There is one aspect of a comprehensive school that can't be measured – the quality of the young people it is producing. This will be my most impressive memory of Creighton. In their concern for tolerance, freedom, equality, fairness and democracy, they are unrecognizable from the pupils of my generation . . . I have no proof, but I am sure they will make better citizens and will strive to make the world a better place.

Our work as teachers in a comprehensive school is often difficult, frustrating and exhausting: it is also rewarding. The outcome which Hunter Davies thought he found at Creighton is the outcome we seek for every child.

7 As I see it

Arnold Jennings
Headmaster, Ecclesfield School, Sheffield

What do you want?

How much discipline?

You cannot decide whether you have got enough discipline (or too much discipline) until you have decided how much discipline you want. Nor can you decide if you have the right kind of discipline until you have decided what kind of discipline you want. There is no one correct answer to either of these questions, both of which admit of a number of different answers. Different people would give different answers; one man's sound, firm discipline is another man's regimentation, turning out unthinking automata. People are entitled to their own opinion in this matter. We cannot prove the other fellow's opinion wrong; we can only show why we do not share it and why we prefer whatever we do prefer. If we are parents, we may well endeavour to see that our children are in a school whose corporate views on this are as close to our own as possible.

A girl of thirteen once entered the school of which I am head as a transfer from a school in another part of the country on account of het parents' removal. After she had been with us a fortnight I asked her how she was settling in. She needed little encouragement to make it clear that she thought her last school had been a much better school. When asked why, she said, 'They did things properly there.' When asked for examples, she said, 'Well, here when you go into school dinner you just go in, collect your things and your dinner and sit down and eat it, then hand in your things and go out; at the last school you formed up in lines, and when the mistress blew a whistle the whole line went in; you waited for her to say "Sit down", then you all sat down.' Different people would have different views about which school's discipline, as exemplified in this instance, they preferred. I had a girl once who had left another school at fifteen, and been at a technical college for two years and then came into our sixth form. Two years later, when I was giving her her A level results, I asked her how she had found it, coming back to school at seventeen after two years away from school. She said, 'I don't think the sixth form here is like being at school.' I was very pleased with this remark, which I took as a compliment to the school. There may be those who would have some hesitation about a school of which such a remark could be made and whose head would take it as a compliment.

What sort of discipline?

There are many different kinds of discipline. One distinction is between the motives that lead a pupil to do what is laid down as part of school discipline that he should do. It can be an automatic action, or an automatic obedient response to an instruction, with no thought of doing anything else. This is similar to the basic element in army or navy discipline. There are other places in life besides the armed forces in which this is a useful quality to possess; there are some where it is irrelevant or a positive hindrance to efficient action.

A pupil can do what a school's discipline requires of him, whilst being very aware of possible alternative actions, which might seem more attractive. He can do this through fear of the punishment, if he does not do this and is found out (sanctions). He can do this because he wishes to win and keep the good opinions of his mentors. He can do this through fear of being different from the others. In communities, such as some boarding schools and some semi-adult training institutions, conformity to the common ideas of the peer group can be the major motive, and the institution may deliberately build on this and use it as a cornerstone to bring about in its pupils or students the ideas, outlook and conduct it wishes.

The pupil may do what is desirable based on a conscious and willing choice from among clearly envisaged alternatives. This again can be either because it is perceived as being the wish of the institution, which the pupil is prepared to accept, at least for as long as he belongs to it, or because apart from any other considerations it is what the pupil himself thinks is the best thing for him to do. The first of these was neatly exemplified when a friend of mine, who was headmaster of a mixed grammar school in a Midlands industrial city, announced in assembly that boys and girls should not walk through the streets holding hands. This got out and was taken up by the local media. A journalist on the local paper asked some senior boys and girls from the school whether they agreed with this, or thought the edict was old-fashioned and unnecessary. Their reply was, 'We do think it's old-fashioned and unnecessary, but the head's a good chap, and if he wants us not to do it, we won't do it' – a reply which greatly pleased the head. The second case, where the pupil chooses the desired course of action voluntarily because he also thinks it is best for him, would seem to most people the ideal situation to aim for. It is Plato's 'truth in the soul', it is the same as the Christian concept of a state of grace. It demands a minimum level of maturity, not only of age, but of moral calibre, including often strength of will. The pupil's view of the best thing for him to do might, in practice, more often coincide with the school's view in matters such as vandalism, honesty or speaking the truth rather than in wearing uniform or smoking (though this last has changed in recent years).

Discipline in what things?

Another distinction between different kinds of discipline is between the areas in which it is considered essential that discipline should exist and be observed and enforced. One school thinks it an essential part of school discipline to prescribe a uniform (which might take different forms with different ages of pupils) and to say what articles of dress may and may not be worn at school; another may take the view that this is not an important matter and that to fight great battles to maintain its enforcement is a misdirection of energy, or may think that given the attitudes of its older pupils it would fit in better with the disciplinary system as a whole which it wishes to see in the school if hard-and-fast rules were not insisted on in this matter, and that this would assist in bringing about the attitude towards school that it wished to see in these pupils, so that they would readily cooperate in other matters which the school thought more important.

In the American army a much more relaxed physical attitude and manner would be considered acceptable in a soldier speaking to a superior in rank than would in the British army or in the Soviet army. All three armies would agree that total discipline in an army is absolutely essential; they would differ in their views and practice in what matters it is necessary for discipline to be observed. A visitor being shown round a Soviet school by its head would find that any girls they met would always curtsey. In England today some teachers would not allow a boy to address them with his hands in his pockets; some other teachers would regard this as out-of-date and unnecessary or even as prejudicial to the kind of good relationships they wished to foster between themselves and their pupils. It is not that one is well-disciplined and the other is 'slack', it is a difference of conception and aim.

Pupils, who are very rarely 'fooled', even when their teachers or parents think they are, have a very sound instinct in this; their standard question is 'are we forced to?' A young teacher might groan at this way of putting it and start explaining that this (whatever it was) was entirely for their own good and prompted solely out of care for them. He would have missed the point that they had seized at once. They were wanting to know if this was one of the matters this school chose to insist upon and permit no deviation, as opposed to the countless things about which their mentors exhorted them to do something, commended it strongly to them, said 'we hope you will all . . .', but left the choice open to, in that nothing would happen to any who did *not*. I have always been happy to answer this question from children, whether 'yes' or 'no', and I think it is helpful if it is made crystal clear to them which are the things that the school, or the teacher, says they *must* do, and means 'must', and which are the things in which in the end they are left with a free choice, no matter how much advice and recommendation they are given. The items on which the school says they *must* do what the school says will differ from

school to school; the difference lies in the school's concept of the kind of discipline it wishes to bring about.

One school might say with pride that its pupils never 'answered back', but accepted the school's authority without question. Another might be equally proud if its pupils, when told to do something, often asked, politely and cheerfully enough, why this was required, and proceeded to discuss it with the teacher, after which, either because they had been convinced that this was a good thing, or because, as in the example above, they said 'we don't think this is necessary or is a good idea, but if the school says we must do it, we suppose we must' and then do it cheerfully enough; the school could say its pupils were intelligent and thoughtful and capable of easy discussion. The difference between the two schools would not be between their success in achieving their disciplinary goals, or that one had higher standards of discipline than the other; it would be between the goals which the two schools set themselves, between the values they chose as being the most important.

How to get it

When you have decided what sort of discipline you want, as well as how much, and where, how do you get it and keep it?

See that your discipline is consistent, that it does not vary according to what sort of day you have been having, or according to how near the start or the end of term it is, or according to which pupil it is, or what kind of pupil, or whether it is a boy or a girl. See that every pupil knows what the discipline is, what the rules are, what is expected of him/her, where the lines are drawn, transgression of which will not be accepted. This does not necessarily mean writing out lists of 'School Rules' and having them up on the wall in every classroom. That is one way, but there are others – frequent telling in school, house, year or form assembly; having one or two copies up in the school and seeing that every pupil knows where they are.

See that discipline is consistent, whoever is applying it, and that every teacher on the staff observes and enforces the same code of discipline. This is harder to obtain than might first be thought. If a teacher profoundly disbelieves in some item in the school's discipline, he/she may not go out of his way or be too punctilious to see that it is maintained. Some will go further and will actively undermine the discipline laid down, in those points in which they do not agree with it. A young teacher, one of the more thoughtful and serious-minded, who thinks that this matters a lot, and that the school's system is wrong, may well in practice follow his own beliefs. Pupils quickly learn from this. They may well learn that corporate systems are not as monolithic as they might wish to appear, and observe carefully in order to note where the rifts are, sometimes even learning how to insert wedges into them and so widen them, to their own immediate advantage. That is not the kind of lesson of life our pupils should be learning in school, and certainly not from practice in this way.

Involve all members of staff in the process of deciding on the disciplinary system, whether in big staff meetings or in smaller groups, or individually in an informal way. See that members of staff have the opportunity if they wish to discuss the school's disciplinary system. A teacher should be helped to come to realize that he is entitled to try to get the system changed, but that if he does not succeed, he must show loyalty, and operate the system, and that it is in the best interests of the children that he should do so. If the system is so repugnant to his own ideas that he cannot bring himself to do this, he should seek a post in another school more congenial to his outlook.

In the same way the school should not fight against its parents, the governors, the LEA or the area. I remember nearly twenty years ago telling a teenage girl she should not have her ears pierced for earrings. She looked at me in obvious surprise and asked, 'Why, what's wrong with it'? I was about to tell her what I thought was wrong with it when I realized that quite possibly her mother had pierced ears, and that any criticism I made would apply equally to the mother so I did not answer. I hope I am wiser now and no longer think that imposing my own tastes on others who do not share them constitutes 'raising standards'. In many cases the curriculum, and often much of the ethos, of a school involves quite enough alienation of a pupil from his environment without adding to it where it is not called for. This is not to say that parental opinion, expressed or assumed, is to be given a veto over what a school does. A school should seek to explain to parents what it is trying to do and to convince them, carry them and win their support. Secondly a school should distinguish between issues that really matter, on which it would be loth to compromise, and issues that are not essential – like earrings. The same principles apply if the head and the staff find that their views on discipline differ from their own governors, or their LEA.

Similarly it helps enormously, if indeed it is not essential, to bring the main body of the pupils of the school as a whole to the state where they accept that the disciplinary system of the school is in the main reasonable and that its enforcement is in practice 'fair'. If this is not the case the school will be in for trouble and will at the very least experience difficulty. It helps, as has been said, to make absolutely certain that it is crystal clear to every pupil exactly what are the things that are regarded as essential and which will be insisted upon (the things they 'are forced' to do), among the welter of advice and recommendations that pupils are surrounded with. Two apparently conflicting principles help here. First it should always be clear that authority is authority and cannot be trifled with or gainsaid in those matters where it has been made clear that this will be the case. No wavering or dithering, no hesitance! Second, it helps if the school tries to explain to pupils the reasons for its discipline, and why various things are laid down. I used to tell pupils in assembly that I would always be glad to listen to any boy or girl who came to ask why we had a particular rule, and that if they could show me and the teaching staff that it served no purpose we would change the rule. (Those who took up this offer and came to see me were few in number and always from the junior forms.)

Schools should aim to involve the parents in school discipline. Besides seeking to explain to parents in general terms the school's disciplinary system, what it is trying to do and how it is trying to do it, and attempting to win their support in this, in dealing with individual pupils teachers should seek to involve the pupil's parents and to work with them if possible. Parents can be written to, rung up and/or invited into school, with or without an appointment, to see a particular teacher either about the pupil's school life in general or about some particular incident. If the parent asks for this it should always be granted with no great delay. If a teacher sets out the facts of a case or a position as he sees them in a tactful and understanding way, and makes clear his basic concern for the pupil, a parent will almost always recognize the teacher's concern for *his* son or daughter and the teacher's professionalism. In those cases where this does not occur nothing is lost except time and sometimes, almost, patience and temper. The cases where the teacher ends up winning the parent's support and cooperation in dealing with the pupil are well worth the far smaller number in which the two sides do little more than agree to differ.

There are a number of factors which will help a school with its discipline. One is a suitable curriculum. This is partly a matter of each pupil's ability, his background, his goals and aims (when he has formulated them), and how particular subject matter is 'put across' in class. Pupils ought not to be left working on a curriculum which they feel is of no relevance or use to them. This may mean altering the curriculum, or its presentation, or, better, seeing that pupils can see what it has to offer to them. If they think, rightly or wrongly, that it has nothing, this will not predispose them to cooperate with the school in other matters.

A good pastoral care system is another enormous help, because it will often see trouble coming before it arrives and enable something to be done to prevent it. It can deal with those who are in difficulties, of whatever kind or source, and by helping them make them less likely to react by kicking over the traces. Similarly, it helps enormously if pupils perceive that their teachers *care* for them, are really concerned for *their* welfare. If teachers are so concerned, they will not need to take any steps to make pupils realize it. Pupils are very perceptive in such matters, and if teachers care for them, 98 per cent of them will perceive that this is so.

Good public relations, in quite general terms, help a school with its discipline. If parents and pupils feel that in general the school is doing the right job and doing it well, pupils will be more disposed to cooperate and parents to support the school in its endeavours. In the days (long gone) when the school I presided over insisted on boys wearing school caps I used to say, 'Every university entry announced means one less parent objecting to our requiring school caps to be worn.' The same could be said of every achievement in games or in social service in the local community.

Buildings and equipment help or hinder. I once inherited as part of an amalgamation a set of buildings which a trendy architect had designed in rough unfinished concrete with the wooden shuttering marks on the concrete being the only decoration. To school children in an industrial city this looks like their idea of a prison. I have had as large an area as possible of the internal grey walls covered with bright paint, either by decorators (I was refused this at the first request as being 'against the architect's conception') or by turning chosen pupils loose on stretches of wall under the guidance of an art teacher. My LEA urges us not to turn on corridor lights unless absolutely necessary, to save fuel costs. I prefer to keep all corridors lit up, bright and cheerful, so that there are no dark and gloomy tunnels for any pupils to go through, in order that this may play its little part in predisposing the pupils to the corresponding feelings (see Plato, *Republic*, Book III). Some pieces of design, and some equipment, invite vandalism; others resist it. It is not a matter of being stoutly made, still less of being plain, but of good and sensible design, and being designed by someone who knows what the inside of a school is like, and its pupils, or who has consulted someone who does.

When anything in the building is vandalized, or damaged by accident, or by fair wear and tear, it should never be accepted and left damaged. It should always be repaired, or graffiti removed or painted over, as soon as possible, so that pupils do not see the example of broken, defaced or damaged equipment or buildings. If it is not known how it happened, an enquiry should always be made. If it is successful, if someone is found to have done it deliberately, he can be punished and/or, more important, perhaps corrected, so that he will be less likely to do it again. If it is unsuccessful and nothing is discovered, at least the pupils know that it is a matter of concern.

It helps, if pupils are not required to move all at once down corridors or stairs that are too narrow to take them all at the same time, if access to lockers is in some place where they will not be constantly brushed aside by other pupils needing to go past. Not all school buildings make this possible, but the school should do its best with the buildings it has and do all it can to minimize the effects of any faults or inadequacies in the buildings. It helps if teachers arrive at each class on time for the beginning of the lesson, or as near to this as the buildings and the school time-table allow. It helps if all written work set is always marked, and comments made to each individual pupil, either orally or in writing on his piece of work. It helps if pupils are always kept reasonably well occupied, and if at lunch time, for example, there is a good range of different kinds of voluntary activities available.

If a potentially explosive situation arises, it helps to defuse it as quickly as possible and not to be stiff-necked and let it run, or even push it, until there is a blow-up. If two people are in a confrontation and tempers are being lost, what matters first is to get them apart and let all concerned cool down, calm down and have time for second thoughts before proceeding to try to resolve whatever issue had led to this situation.

Extreme cases
All this may perhaps sound fine, but does it work? It would be miraculous if it worked for every pupil in every school all the time. This, or discipline obtained by similar means to those outlined, or by an appropriate variation of them, works with nearly all pupils nearly all the time. The incidence of this is uneven; some schools have no difficulties or trouble with discipline, others have a good deal. Some are of course in much more difficult situations than others. The buildings the school is in, the nature of the area it draws its pupils from, the amount of support it can attract from its parents and from its surrounding area, the expectations its pupils can reasonably entertain are obvious factors which make an enormous difference. A grammar school in a stockbroker belt or a leafy suburb starts from a totally different baseline from a secondary modern in dilapidated and overcrowded buildings in dockland or an inner-city ghetto. Those who wish to compare schools' achievements publicly should also compare what they start from, and what they have going for them or the reverse, what factors there are making for the school's success or the opposite, and should then try to estimate how far the school has got from what it started with, allowing for these factors, and judge its achievements on that basis.

There will be individual cases in most schools where the school discipline fails. If this is in major matters rather than minor, and if there are certain pupils who are repeatedly in this position, special measures may be necessary. Obviously the school will have special measures of a simple and elementary kind which are available when a pupil's behaviour appears to call for them, such as being put 'on report' – presenting a card, or book, to a series of teachers throughout the week for a written report on the pupil's conduct, if necessary in each lesson, the card then to be taken to the head, house-master, year-master or whatever at the end of the week for appropriate action. I am thinking of those cases in which the school has been through every special measure it has in its repertoire with a particular pupil, whose behaviour continues to be such as to be unacceptable – persistent and constant pilfering, violence to other pupils, sustained defiance of staff and violence offered to them, constant disruption of lessons to an extent that normal teaching cannot take place, constant truancy or constant unnecessary absence known and condoned by the parents.

If the school has done all it can and the result is still unacceptable, two things can then be done. One is to call in help from outside the school and see if others can succeed where the school could not – education welfare officers ('the attendance man'), educational psychiatrists, 'school liaison officers', and social workers of various kinds. They can sometimes achieve what the school could not. They are not likely to do this, however, unless they and the school work together in the closest cooperation.

If this does not succeed, I am among the growing number who say that in the interests both of the pupil concerned, to correct him if possible, but in any case to limit his opportunity for getting into further trouble, and of the other pupils in the school, he should be removed from the environment in which he is causing unacceptable trouble – which may be the classroom, or even some teachers' lessons (but not others'), or perhaps the whole environment of the school throughout the day, until there is reason to hope that he can take a normal place in it again without behaving in an unacceptable way. This does *not* necessarily mean that he is sent home and left without any education, even for a short time. Many schools are now setting up special units within the school to contain and cope with – and educate – such pupils. This may be in the charge of a designated member of staff good at this kind of work, or may be shared between a number; it may have a room or suite of its own, or in some cases it has separate premises on the school site. A pupil may be there for a number of periods each week, or for the whole of the week; he may stay there two days, two weeks, or two terms. Whilst he is there he should receive specialist attention from those efficient in this kind of work, and his own education should continue. The aim should not be punitive but to return him to the normal class as soon as possible, and meanwhile to contain him in such a way as to preclude further cases of the behaviour which led to his being there. We have such a unit in my own school, which has 2,000 pupils; sometimes it is not needed for a term at a time, as there are no pupils for whom it is called for, sometimes it has one pupil in it, sometimes two or three, never more than five or six and rarely so many. It is officially known in school by the name of the teacher in charge of it, as 'Mr – 's group', and is always referred to to the children as 'You'd better go with Mr – .' This makes some demand on resources, chiefly accommodation, and heavy demands on staffing; some LEAs are more helpful than others in this regard.

There will be the occasional pupil who either needs specialist expert treatment which a school cannot provide using its own staff and within its own resources, or whom the school cannot contain, in the sense indicated above, even in such a unit. A boy who is aggressive and who manifests this by seizing other pupils and, apparently, half-throttling them, and whom the school is unable to prevent from doing this from time to time, should not be left among the other pupils at all. For a school to guarantee this would necessitate its setting up almost prison conditions, or at least the equivalent of army 'close arrest', either of which would seem unreasonable and hardly describable as being 'at school'. For such pupils I think the LEA should maintain its own special centre, appropriately sited, equipped and staffed; some do, and the number is growing. Some LEAs send such pupils home and employ teachers to travel round teaching them in their homes ('home tuition'), as they do in some cases of illness or handicap.

Checks on the teacher; support for the teacher

When a teacher in maintaining discipline has occasion to punish a pupil in some way, the pupil's parents may well sometimes wonder if the punishment was really merited or was 'fair', especially as they may at this stage only have heard their son's or daughter's account of what happened and what led up to it, which may not always be a wholly balanced or a completely accurate account. The parent should, on such occasions, always get in touch with the teacher – who will often be wise to communicate with the parents without waiting for this – and hear his or her account of what happened. There may be occasions when after this the parent still feels aggrieved and that justice has not been done. In such cases it should be possible for the parents to raise the matter, as it should with anything else that happens in school. This should first be with the teacher's head; if this does not lead to any change in the parent's feelings, and he thinks it important enough to warrant it, he should then approach the teacher's LEA. It should then be possible for the matter to be looked into, if it seems that this would be justified, by an impartial, responsible and competent person. An LEA adviser or other appropriate officer, or if necessary HMI, would seem suitable. This person could then tell each side of the dispute, or difference in opinion, the rights and wrongs and merits of the case as he saw them. This could apply to other incidents or events in school, for example if a parent thought his son was being unfairly treated in some way in the teaching or the organization of the school, and it should be the same with discipline. This would give the parent the opportunity to raise the issue and have it looked into, and the teacher the opportunity for this to be done by a competent, responsible and appropriate person. It should not be the case that in the single case of corporal punishment a teacher, endeavouring to do his duty as well as he is able, can find himself in a law court as the accused person, on a charge of assault. Lawyers tell us that no teacher who has administered moderate and reasonable corporal punishment (and 'reasonable' includes the circumstances, and the offence, as well as the punishment itself) ever need fear conviction. But the teacher should not have to appear in court on a criminal charge, even if – all the more if – he is then acquitted. The procedure suggested could deal with all cases. If there are cases such as the opponents of corporal punishment tell us exist, where sadistic teachers exercise immoderate and unreasonable corporal punishment, even where there is no justification for any punishment, this would come to light under such a procedure and could be adequately and fully dealth with, according to whatever turned out to be the facts.

Parents and their children, the pupils, are entitled to safeguards, and to checks that are effective in that if something is wrong it can be and will be dealt with. Teachers are entitled to support where they are doing their job efficiently and adequately, sometimes under very trying and difficult circumstances. Society, here as elsewhere, is often ready enough to will the end but reluctant to will the necessary means. If discipline in some schools is too lax, as some popularists constantly claim in their jeremiads against the world today, teachers who endeavour to maintain it should receive every support – even if society is represented by a member of a governing body or an education committee, who has the complaining parent as a neighbour, a friend, or a constituent, or all three.

A few years ago, in front of the whole class, a fifteen-year-old boy hit a woman teacher, who was in her first term out of college as a young probationer, sufficiently hard to knock her down on the floor. When this was later reported to the governors of that school, the first comment made was by a governor who said 'Whatever had she done to provoke the boy into doing such a thing?'

Checks on schools

It is no more true of the teaching profession than of any other that every one of its members is an apostle of sweetness and light and 100 per cent successful all the time. Some are better and more efficient than others. It has also already been pointed out that some schools start with many more difficulties than others. It should not surprise us therefore if different schools achieve different levels of success in their discipline – indeed what is surprising is that the standards are as even as they are across schools as a whole, and are as high as they are, according to the testimony of unbiassed observers such as school inspectors, national or local who are in a position to know. However, anyone is entitled to ask if they are high enough in general or in a particular school. In the maintained schools the system provides for this, by providing a mechanism to check it. It should not be forgotten that there could be concern that a school's discipline was far too severe and tight, or that it was being applied in wrong or in-appropriate areas, just as much as there could be concern that it was too lax, or was not being applied to areas where it was felt that it should.

The LEA has its inspectors and advisers, who should know their schools anyway and have a fair idea of what they are doing – unless the LEA is using its advisers and inspectors to do a thousand and one odd jobs other than advising and inspecting. Schools have their bodies of governors, and there is an education committee. Any suggestion that a school is failing in this (or anything else) and that something should be done about it can be taken up by the LEA, if it is satisfied there appear to be sufficient grounds. Its advisers can then look into the matter and report their findings to the LEA, which can then either announce that it is satisfied that all is well, or can proceed to appropriate discussions with the school about how to put right what is considered to be wrong.

70

8 A primary head speaks

Peter Kennedy
Headmaster, Great Wakering Primary School, Essex

There is a temptation to begin this chapter with a definition of discipline. However, it is a temptation which can be easily resisted since it would put me in competition with many distinguished educationists, so I shall describe my beliefs in simple terms. This description is necessary because views on the subject of discipline in schools today should be measured against the writer's attitude to what is an acceptable level of behaviour in a school.

In a primary school where children's ages range from five to eleven it is the adults who decide that there are some things which the children may do and others which they may not; that there are places and times where they may run about and skip and shout, and others where they may do none of these things. These do's and don'ts may be codified into a set of school rules (perhaps for presentation to the managing body) but the children will be made aware of them and reminded of them from time to time by word of mouth.

The rules will have been evolved, amended and discussed at staff meetings although it is highly probable that, in the main, they will have been made as a result of the head teacher's suggestions. The underlying principle will be simple and straightforward: that the school should be a place where children can work hard, a place where they can be happy and a place where, as far as is humanly possible, they can be safeguarded from injury. When children are reminded of them, these rules will always be related to the reason for their existence. Most primary children are able to distinguish between rules laid down for their own wellbeing and those evolved from the philosophy of 'Go and see what the children are doing and tell them to stop it', particularly if they are helped in the way suggested in the previous sentence.

They will understand that a child struggling to grasp a mathematical concept is going to have to struggle that much harder if others in the class are allowed to shout across the room to one another so the teacher must be the arbiter of how much noise may be allowed at a particular time. They will realize that school life is not going to be enjoyed by all, if teachers do nothing to prevent a child from punching others or interfering with their playtime games. They will be aware that both work and pleasure are going to be temporarily suspended for the child whose leg is broken because the rules regulating movement up and down staircases have not been enforced.

I hope these simple examples illustrate what I understand by discipline in primary schools. A great deal of this will, of course, be self-discipline because children are not always in sight of teachers. A school where the relevant rules were obeyed most of the time by most of the children I would regard as well-disciplined, therefore efficient, happy and safe. One where such rules did not exist or were persistently flouted I would regard as ill-disciplined, unhappy and unsafe.

The restrictions on children's absolute freedom which I have indicated are similar to those many of us would apply to our own children in our homes. We would not allow younger children to play table-tennis in the room where their sister was studying for O levels. And she, when she had finished her homework, would be discouraged from playing her radio at full blast because it would keep the younger children awake and disturb the neighbours.

It must also be said that, in the school, as in the home, the rules which impose discipline are generally made without much consideration of their psychological or sociological implications. They are 'convenience rules' and may be altered from time to time as circumstances change. But, since they all relate to things that the children can understand, namely, the need to work, their personal safety, and their opportunity to enjoy life, they have the virtue that they do not appear to be rules made simply for the sake of having rules.

If the general observance of this code of conduct results in a well-disciplined school then that observance is the result of work on the part of the teachers who have to be aware of the rules and the reasons for their existence. Once members of staff are agreed on the level of behaviour to be expected from children it will be by their efforts that the level will be attained and maintained.

The way in which these efforts are directed has not altered much during my time in the teaching profession. It depends greatly upon the ability of teachers to agree on certain lines of action; for instance, it is still as necessary as it ever was for teachers to prepare their lessons carefully. Children of primary school age seldom behave badly in class when there is plenty of purposeful work for them to do and thus the danger of an ill-disciplined classroom is averted. It is also important that all teachers (including, of course, the head teacher) be determined that the children will understand that they are being fairly treated. In apportioning blame for misbehaviour, no teacher will act upon the uncorroborated word of another child, or of a group of children, and this will be made clear to the child who is accused of a misdemeanour. The word of a teacher or of another adult (such as a midday dinner assistant), to whom responsibility is delegated will, of course, normally be accepted by the head even against the most vehement denial on the part of the child. Overall, however, the head must convey to the children the knowledge that they will not be punished in a capricious manner without a reasonable investigation into all the relevant circumstances.

In the maintenance of a reasonable level of behaviour, no school can afford to fail to involve the parents. Parental involvement, in this instance, is not merely a matter of the *rights* of parents to know what goes on at the school their children attend but it is also a matter of their *responsibility* for the behaviour of the children who are sent to school. Once a head has satisfied himself that all that he can reasonably expect is being done within the school to deal with a child who persistently behaves badly, he needs to discuss the matter with the parents or guardians to ensure that they are cooperating with the school in its efforts to put matters to rights.

This interview with the parents will have been preceded by careful discussion between the head, the class teacher and with any other teacher who has something to say about the behaviour problem of the child in question and also a discussion with the child. In other words, there has emerged in the primary school a system similar to the counselling system which operates in many secondary schools. The primary school, however, suffers the grave disadvantage that, as a general rule, the staffing formula allows for one teacher per class and does not allow for non-teaching periods. The result is that the class teacher has not the time during school hours to talk to the difficult child and try to understand the causes of misbehaviour. The choice then becomes one between seeing the child at playtime, or after school, and the alternative of leaving the counselling to the head teacher. The danger of the former is that a genuine attempt to help him may seem to the child to be a punishment ('stay in at playtime' or 'see me after school') while the difficulty of the latter is that the head will, in a sense, be dealing with the problem at second hand both when talking to the child and when reporting his observations to the teacher. Makeshift arrangements can be, and frequently are, made by having the head take the class to free the teacher for counselling but a busy head who already has a full timetable of educational, administrative and teaching duties is a poor substitute for a staffing formula which would allow regular non-teaching periods to primary teachers for marking, preparation, and a chance to talk to children as individuals.

Those who are opposed to corporal punishment and who wonder why it has not completely disappeared from all primary schools might like to reflect that it is still used occasionally because the staff simply do not have time for the other alternatives. In those circumstances a persistent bully, or a disobedient and disruptive child may be, as a last resort, smacked as much for the protection of the other children as for any other reason and the sad fact is that, within those terms, it usually works. It may not get to the basic causes of the child's misbehaviour but it will often ensure a period of peace for those he has tormented, or a change in the working atmosphere of the class which he has disrupted. The good secondary schools which have genuinely abolished all corporal punishment have replaced it, very successfully, with talk – only it is called counselling. Because of their much lower levels of staffing, it is a shame that primary schools are deprived of the opportunity to use talk not only in place of corporal punishment, but also instead of the other arid forms of deprivation to which they are driven as an alternative. I am not advocating the termination of all forms of punishment within a school, but I am arguing that punishment alone seldom helps a child personally.

Although with the vast majority of children major disciplinary problems will not arise, there will always be a minority who present a special problem. Indeed, from the point of view of discipline one could divide children into three groups. By far the largest group would be those children who will normally respond to good teaching in a happy school where they feel cared for. The second and much smaller group will include children who are less willing than the majority to accept the rules of the school but who can be helped without too much difficulty except that of finding time for the classteacher to counsel them. The third group is so small that in any one year many primary schools will not have such a pupil on roll, namely the severely disturbed or maladjusted child.

Children in the second and third groups can, at their varying levels, be described as having behaviour problems and they exhibit behaviour problems whatever their age. We do the children no service and we do secondary schools no service if we persist in regarding infant and junior children as presenting a different and lesser kind of difficulty from children of secondary age, for to do so is to put too much emphasis on physical control of the child by the teacher.

A primary school head teacher may feel that he has less reason than his secondary colleagues to worry about the unruly child, since he is confident of always being able physically to restrain any child of primary age, no matter how violent he or she might become. Statements to this effect are not often made explicitly but the idea is often implicit in remarks about disciplinary difficulties. The trouble with this kind of thinking is two-fold. In the first place, if it were carried to its logical conclusion, one would be forced to argue that the only teachers capable of dealing with badly behaved children in the secondary school would be those who are skilled in the martial arts, and in the second place it allows the education system to ignore the need to give special help to disruptive children at whatever age their difficulties may be diagnosed.

So, in the primary school, how should we deal with the children in my two smaller groups? For those in the second group (the minority, who are less willing than the majority to respond to reasonable school rules), I have indicated my view that they could be greatly assisted by improved staffing in primary schools and, I would add, by the greater availability of experts in the supportive services such as educational psychologists.

The third group, although so small, needs further consideration. Children in this group are not easily helped even by sympathetic and enlightened discussion with teachers. Even the most experienced and skilled teachers find that the presence of such a severely disturbed child in a class makes unfair demands on the teacher's time to the disadvantage of the other children in the class, and the head teacher, in his efforts both to help the child and to deal with the problems brought about by his behaviour within the school, is obliged to give a disproportionate amount of his time and attention to only one of the children for whose education he is responsible.

For reasons which will be suggested later, I believe that the numbers of children in Groups 2 and 3 have increased over the years. This is perhaps of less significance in the case of the children in the second group but it is of some importance in the case of the very disturbed children. I have no doubt that for their own sakes and for the sake of all the others in the school, this group is in need of some form of special education. To those who would argue that they should always be educated within the normal school system I would point out that to do so effectively would be a very expensive solution. It would demand a pupil–teacher ratio so favourable as to be far superior to that operated by even the most generous local education authority in this country. This would be essential if the time which teachers should give to helping children with severe behaviour problems (and helping, in most of the cases, their parents), is not to be filched from the time which they owe to the majority of children within the school. Even if the staffing ratio were improved to that extent, grave doubts would still exist in many minds as to the ability of all teachers in the ordinary schools to deal with the unusual problems of the disturbed child as effectively as do their colleagues now in special education. At the moment there are two places where these children may be helped: there is the school for maladjusted children and there is a newer development, the special unit in which small groups of disruptive children are taught by teachers anxious to help them, in classrooms which are usually on the campus of a normal day school and which generally come under the control of the head of that school. There is, of course, a difference in the operation of each of these institutions. In the recognized school for maladjusted children the pupils are often (to a large extent), separated from their peers in ordinary schools. On the other hand, the children who attend a special unit, while they enjoy the advantage of being taught in small groups by specialist teachers, are also able to take part in many of the activities of the school to which the unit is attached.

In an ideal situation there would be a difference between the school for maladjusted children and the special unit, with the former catering for more severely disturbed children than the latter. In practice, because of the variation in provision, a child who, under one local authority, might be educated in a school for maladjusted children could find himself, if he lived in another part of the country, being catered for by a special unit or perhaps by the normal provisions of a normal school. Surely there should be a clearer distinction between the roles of these two institutions? The school for maladjusted children should educate those children who had been identified as being in need of special education by the procedures laid down by the Department of Education and Science, or, preferably, by a new streamlined form of those procedures. If, at the same time, provision was made for an adequate number of places in schools for maladjusted children, the need for special units could well disappear. If they were still felt to be needed, and many of them have proved their usefulness at the present level of provision, they might well cope with the disturbed children who were not maladjusted but still presented a major problem in the ordinary school.

To the teachers in a primary school who have identified a child as being so disturbed as to require specialist help of one kind or another, the amount of time and effort that has to be put into obtaining that help is a constant source of frustration. Time, rather than effort, is the main cause of frustration because it results in the continuation of the situation in which so many other children are deprived of their fair share of the teacher's attention.

There are the hours spent within the school talking to, reasoning with, and punishing the more flagrant misdeeds of the disturbed child. There is the time spent discussing the problem with the parents who may genuinely seek assistance with the problem or who, as often occurs, may argue that what appears to teachers and the parents of other children as outrageous behaviour on the part of their child, is merely the naughtiness of the normal boy or girl. Then, when the educational psychologist is involved, much of this has to be gone over again before and after the tests are administered and before further advice is given to the school. When eventually it is agreed that specialist help is essential in the situation, there will probably be a long wait before a place can be found in a suitable establishment.

It may seem, to the reader who has persevered thus far, that I have written an unduly large number of words about a group of children who, on my own admission, constitute a tiny minority of the pupils who pass through a primary school. I have done so for three reasons. As I have already stated, I am concerned about the unfair demand such children make upon the time and resources available to teachers who are striving to meet the needs of the slow learner, the average child, the above-average child and the gifted child. I am concerned too about the effects that the misbehaviour of the disturbed child can have upon the more easily led among the children who present the kind of behaviour problems, which it would be reasonable to expect teachers to cope with in the normal day to day running of the school. But, most of all, I am concerned at the failure of primary schools to help the severely disturbed children to recover from their disabilities.

A handful of such children have passed through my own school during the years during which I have been its head. I believe that my colleagues, who spent so much time and patience in trying to help them, would agree that such success as we had was limited to 'containing' them and to attempting to protect the interests of the other children in the school.

As for the disturbed children themselves, they went on to the secondary schools still showing all the emotional and behavioural problems which had manifested themselves in the primary school, and, to the best of my knowledge, many of them went out into the working world with these difficulties unresolved.

Having regard to the size of primary classes today, two things need to be done in this matter. First, and more obviously, more places in special education should be provided so that teachers can work with these children in very small groups. Second, the whole process of assessing the needs of the severely disturbed pupil should be simplified and speeded up. Since the difficulties of this tiny minority of children can often be identified at an early age, one way of speeding up the assessment procedures would be to pay more regard to the opinions of the teachers in the schools.

When I look more broadly at the question of discipline in schools today I see many encouraging signs. The relationship between teacher and pupils is often more friendly and relaxed than perhaps was the case in earlier days and this relationship frequently ensures that children, like their teachers, accept the need for reasonable standards of behaviour and the observance, most of the time, of reasonable school rules.

The relationship between schools and parents has also improved because of the recognition on both sides that they share a common objective, the education and wellbeing of the children. Teachers, for their part, have generally shown a willingness to dismantle such barriers as existed to prevent parents knowing what went on in their children's school. This was probably helped by the post-war influx of married women into the teaching profession, women who were anxious to accord to parents of the children they taught, the same level of information and discussion which they expected to receive from the schools which their own children attended.

There can be little question that a good understanding between parents and teachers can be of great help in dealing with matters related to discipline, just as it can be helpful in dealing with matters related to educational progress. A child who finds he can get away with it will attempt to play off one parent against another and he may also attempt to play the school off against the home. A reasonable level of consultation can avoid this and serve to convince the child that parents and teachers are united in their efforts to enable him to become a happy and helpful member of the school community.

However, alongside these encouraging developments there are others which make the maintenance of a good level of discipline in school more difficult. Let me mention some of them, not attempting to place them in any order of importance.

The increase in the divorce rate means that in every school there are now many more children coming to school from homes with only one parent.

The limited spread within society of an attitude of mind which criticizes or rejects authority ensures that some young children (certainly more than was the case a generation ago) are brought up by their parents, at best in an atmosphere which can be described as anti-authority, at worst, in a home where they are actively encouraged to resist authority.

The consciousness that we are living in a more violent society persuades some parents to instruct their children to use their fists readily the instant they feel threatened – not a new phenomenon, but one which can be observed more frequently than in the past.

In this sexually permissive age, it is not unusual to learn that some parents leave around the house the most explicit sex magazines without making any attempt to conceal them from their children, an attitude towards parental responsibility which surprises many teachers.

Whereas less than a generation ago, primary children might have paid a weekly visit to the cinema to be thrilled by the ritualized violence of the Western or Tarzan, the child of today can be excited at home almost any evening by a very realistic form of violence portrayed in television programmes.

It would be foolish to exaggerate the effects of these or other changes in attitude upon the disciplinary problems of a primary school. After all, I wrote earlier that the largest group of children in such a school contains those who will normally respond to good teaching in a happy school where they feel cared for. I know this to be true and I am aware that some of the children within that majority group will have been subjected to some of the influences which I have listed above and will not appear to have suffered any adverse effects.

But it would be even more foolish to pretend that in discussing the subject of discipline in schools today, these alterations in attitudes can be ignored. A fair amount of research has been done into the effects upon children of some of these developments but, since this is the expression of a personal point of view, I do not intend to quote from research findings, and I merely make the following comments, drawing on my own experience.

To reinforce my statement that I have not placed the above points in any order of merit or demerit, I shall deal with them in reverse order.

It is difficult to assess the effect upon children of watching scenes of violence on television but one particular aspect of it has been noted by several teachers. About ten or twelve years ago I remember saying to a class of children about a playground fight, 'and what made it worse was this. After the boy had been pushed to the ground the others actually started to kick him.' This statement drew from the children the gasps of horror and disbelief which I had hoped for. Today, some infant children come to school conditioned in the belief that 'putting the boot in' is a method of fighting used by villains and heroes alike. This behaviour does not present a major problem that cannot be coped with in school but it indicates perhaps the effect on the young mind of violence on the screen at home.

It would no doubt be argued by some experts that it is a healthy sign when children can share with parents their enjoyment of the photographs in 'girlie' magazines and, as their reading ability improves, share their interest in the accompanying letters and articles. However, this tolerance does not yet extend to most parents and most teachers who expect the head to discourage the children from bringing such magazines to school, and head teachers have a duty to bear this reasonable expectation in mind. Once again it must be made clear that there is no suggestion that the permissive attitude is widely prevalent but this is another small indication of the changed social climate within which a school must enforce its discipline. The head will still not allow sex magazines to be shown to all the children in the school but, in talking to the offender, he can no longer assume that the child's parents will necessarily support his strictures. This also applies to the school's teaching about truthfulness and honesty, as witness for example, the increasing number of cases in which parents condone truancy.

The increasing encouragement of children in the belief that it is a tough world and so they must be ready to react to any threats from other children by using their fists (and their feet and their finger nails) also makes it more difficult for the primary school to enforce its rules by reason alone. The primary teacher can no longer assume that all, save a tiny minority of parents, will support the school in discouraging children from taking the law into their own hands. More often than was previously the case, parents will say, 'Perhaps I'm to blame that he's like that. I've always told him not to be afraid to "have a bundle" if anyone was getting at him.' Where the school fails to persuade the parents that it is the teachers' job to deal with attacks, real or imagined, on their children, the system of discipline suffers because children can see that two sets of adults, their parents and their teachers, hold opposing views on a subject of vital importance to them. It is worth noting that, in many schools, this difficulty is minimised by a simple matter of communication. Where a child goes home bearing a bruise, a cut, a scratch or wearing an article of clothing which has been torn, he takes home a letter. This informs the parents that the incident has been investigated and that it was the result of a genuine accident, or, where this is not so, that the other child concerned has been suitably dealt with. Parents are thus reassured that in school their children will be protected by the rules of the school and that there is no need for the children to feel that they should dispense summary justice.

The slowly increasing evidence of the growth of an anti-authority attitude poses fairly obvious problems for the school and the most serious of these is that it presents yet another instance where the child is confused by seeing that his parents and his teachers hold opposing points of view. When it arises this is a difficulty which could often be resolved by discussion between the teachers, the child and the parents were it not for the constraints imposed by the availability of time. In mathematics a child cannot go on discovering year after year that four fives are twenty. There comes a time when he has to memorize it as a fact. In the same way, he has to accept as a fact, that his immediate authority figures – the teachers – are going to make decisions and impose restrictions which he, as a member of the school community, will have to accept as part of the rules of the school designed to help his education and ensure his happiness and safety. The parent who wishes to question every disciplinary decision made by the school staff will also have to accept that fact.

Finally, among this list of things which have made more difficult the maintenance of good discipline, comes the one which was, in a random manner, listed first, namely the growth in the divorce rate and the consequent increase in the number of children from single-parent homes. Any experienced teacher will confirm that many children from broken homes are happy, industrious, well-adjusted members of the school community who appear to have suffered very little, or even not to have suffered at all, from the fact that their parents are separated. At the same time no one can fail to be aware of the severe stress and strain both emotional and economic that are often imposed upon single-parent homes and that at times these stresses and strains manifest themselves in the behaviour of the children as well as in that of the parent. Some of these children will present problems of behaviour in school, and this could well make discipline in schools more difficult to maintain.

The views presented in this chapter are, I believe, realistic and reasonably optimistic. Primary schools, with their almost universal insistence on work in the basic subjects, are clearly not training grounds for junior denizens of a blackboard jungle. Most teachers and most parents accept the need for disciplinary standards in schools which will allow children to be educated in happy and safe conditions. The changes in our society may have brought new problems to schools but given the levels of staffing which it is now reasonable to expect and given the willingness of teachers and parents to be frank and cooperate with one another for the benefit of the children, most of these problems can be solved.

With these conditions and with adequate provision in special education for the severely disturbed children, primary schools could play an even more successful role in eliminating some of the disciplinary problems that can arise in the later stages of a child's education. This belief should bring some comfort but it would be as foolish to be too optimistic about the generally beneficial effects of satisfactory discipline in school as it would to be too pessimistic about behaviour levels in most schools. The school is the minor influence on a child's behavioural development, the home the major one. A child may be encouraged to conform to the rules of the school but if he is unfortunate enough to have parents who, for example, allow him to stay out late in the evenings with no knowledge of his whereabouts, then, in most cases, it will be the home influence that prevails. In other words one is obliged to conclude with a cautionary note and a statement of the obvious.

It is right to be concerned about how children behave at school but wrong to suggest that in good school discipline alone lies the answer to the problems of what many see as an increasingly violent society.

9 A gamekeeper reminisces on his poaching days

Tom Rolf

Senior Adviser for Secondary Education, Devon LEA

One cannot really talk about discipline in schools today without first considering what discipline was like in schools yesterday. I went to a relatively sound boys' grammar school in the suburbs of Manchester, in 1937. As an under-age scholarship winner I was placed in the lowest of three streams. Perhaps, therefore, we did not always get the teachers with the highest standards of discipline, but in my early years in the school we never had less than two teachers per year whose life we made an absolute misery. They were good men and in reality we liked them but, nevertheless, we were very cruel to them. When the war came, and we returned from evacuation to Manchester, we had women teachers in the school and that was too good an opportunity to miss. There was some vandalism committed in the school but it was more of the thoughtless than the deliberate kind. The biro and felt-tip pen had not yet been invented. One of my contemporaries at that time had a propensity for fighting the teachers whom he thought were degrading him. I witnessed two of his three famous ten-minute fights when, with no holds barred, his sturdy five-foot frame, feet flailing, threw itself against teachers, irrespective of their powers of discipline. We did not think of him as being disturbed, although we did think of him as being a bit different from us. I was pleased for his sake when some years later he became Chairman of the Old Boys' Association.

Coincidentally, my own teaching career was to begin in 1952 in a similar kind of school in Lincolnshire. I believe that the overall discipline in that school was better than the school I had attended as a boy but, nevertheless, there were levels of noise in some classrooms which the critics of present day disciplinary standards would claim had never existed in the past. Whenever the opportunity has presented itself the more able child has always been more capable of destroying a lesson, sometimes in a cruel and heartless fashion, rather than the less able child who may opt for a quieter existence which ignores the teacher. The form of which I was form master had a temporary teacher for a period of time whose standard of teaching was very weak. Within a fortnight my form had designed several 'wanted' posters which had a recognizable drawing of the poor man and the charge underneath that he was wanted for fraud, insofar as he purported to be a teacher and was therefore obtaining money under false pretences,

The school which I attended as a child and the school where I was to begin my teaching career had one thing in common. There were many teachers who had been in those schools for a considerable period of time and who were known by their nicknames, mainly of an affectionate kind. Since, in some cases, they had been teaching for as much as thirty years in the same school, the whole community would be capable of swapping anecdotes about the same individuals, even though the ages of the people involved in the swapping could differ considerably. Parents and children would have a common bond in that they had been taught by the same teacher. The strengths and the weaknesses of the teachers were passed on from generation to generation but in the telling of the story the good points normally received publicity. So, although a man may have had weakish discipline it was known that provided you worked he got you through examinations. Therefore, despite the noise level in his lessons, effective work was being done.

When I moved to a West Riding comprehensive school in the late 1950s as a head of department I feared the worst. I had made the move on idealistic grounds but I was apprehensive about the confrontation that I was sure would follow in the classroom when I met children of lower ability, particularly those of the opposite sex. I realized that my standard of discipline might not automatically be of the highest order just because I was over six feet tall, a footballer and a reasonably good teacher. The time span of concentration of the less able pupils was much less than the time span to which I had been accustomed. Also, by my standards, there was not the same initial response to my commands. I had been used to having thirty-two pairs of eyes focused on me whenever it was obvious that I was about to pass on some particular words of wisdom. Now, I had to work harder at my craft, giving more thought to the appropriateness of a particular course of action and the consequences that might follow if I made a mess of what I was doing. In other words, I now had to consider the implications of what I was doing with thirty-two individuals. Incidentally, the same children about whom I was apprehensive were, subsequently, to tell their form mistress that I was 'ever so strict'. Hitherto, I had not had to think too seriously about the content of my subject syllabus. A man called Durell had decreed what was appropriate for the first three years in a grammar school and the examining boards had decided upon the contents of the fourth and fifth years. Now, for the first time, I began to realize the importance of making the content of my subject appropriate to the needs of the child. Even though the school was led by a talented head teacher we did not always get the curriculum for the average and below average pupils which would have fitted their needs. Schools have worked hard on this in the intervening years but it still remains a problem. I don't think it is just a question of making the subjects more vocational or more academic. Children of lower ability must feel that the school cares about their curriculum. That means that they must have a more than equal share of the talented teachers capable of maintaining excellent order within the classroom.

Over the years, and it may be due to failings of my own, I gained the impression that the maintenance of good order and the establishment of good relationships with a class at the beginning of the year became more difficult and more time consuming. The class always seemed to be slightly more inattentive and noisier than in the previous year. Yet, within a month, one's relationships with the children became every bit as good as they had ever been. Respect for the teacher is not now automatic, it has to be earned. Naturally, the changes in attitude which have taken place in schools have closely paralleled the changes of attitude that have taken place in society. No longer, and quite rightly so, is it the practice for children to remain perfectly quiet at the dining table, nor do they have to remain silent in the company of adults until they have been spoken to. Children nowadays will not give their respect or loyalty to an adult, at home or in the school, until that adult has earned it.

In the early 1960s I moved to the deputy headship of a London comprehensive school. I am confident that the disciplinary standards at that time were inferior to the standards of today. The reasons were fairly obvious. It was a time of great teacher shortage and a time when the expense of living in the London area was becoming obvious to most young teachers who had taught for a year or two. Had schools not had a dedicated core of seasoned and hardened professionals in their middle years of teaching then the end result could have been much more serious than it was. I can remember at least two probationary teachers who commenced their teaching at 9 a.m. on the first day of term and gave up teaching at twelve noon on that day. There was an unevenness of quality too amongst the teachers who presented themselves for supply work. Some did very well, but others often created far greater problems by their presence than they would have done had the classes been left unattended. I well remember one particular supply teacher describing his class to their faces as 'a smelly lot of boys'. As a result of this the head had to deal with a set of complaining North-London parents who knew that whatever the faults of their children, one thing they weren't was 'smelly'. My head teacher, a man most adept at making people feel they were valued, used to say that one or two of his best appointments at that time were made in the buffet at Waterloo Station, usually Australians getting off the boat train. As well as the core of talented teachers to whom I have referred, the school also had a reassuring core of pupils dedicated to the good of the school, particularly those of Asian origin. Thus the school got by more than adequately, considering that we were at that time in competition with many neighbouring grammar schools. Regrettably, however, the one per cent of pupils within the school who had behavioural problems, which were often beyond the control of the school, caused great concern to the staff and the school. Even though since that time I have taught and observed teaching in more salubrious areas of the country I have found that there is still a percentage of pupils who can, by the very nature of their problems, present schools with almost insuperable difficulties.

In the middle 1960s I was very fortunate to return as head teacher to the West Riding comprehensive school at which I had been a head of department. The school was uncreamed, possessed a viable and vigorous sixth form and was in an area where house prices were relatively low. There was no shortage of applicants for teaching posts except in those subjects in which there was a national shortage of teachers. All schools, whether they are situated in a semi-rural urban part of Yorkshire, or in the inner areas of London, or in country districts such as Devon have problems which are not totally different in kind. Whenever a local authority deliberately or inadvertently gathers together its problem tenants in one council estate then the school in closest proximity will have problems of a particular kind. It is my feeling, however, that in the final analysis children respond in a not too dissimilar fashion in whatever part of the country they live. It may be that the children of Islington permit a teacher five minutes to prove his worth, whereas West Riding children give five lessons and children from Cullompton give five weeks, but if a teacher fails to impress then the end result will be similar whatever the part of the country. I have always felt it is important for a school to serve a definable area, an area containing a true cross-section of people proportionately gathered from all socio-economic classes. It is much easier to develop a sense of community within the neighbourhood of the school in a semi-rural/urban area than it is in a city area where one may be sharing a neighbouring community with any of four or five other schools. In such instances genuine identification with the community is very difficult. Although the school of which I was head was purpose-built, served a recognizable community and existed in circumstances that were reasonably favourable, we still had our one per cent of disturbed children. The effect they could have upon the school was dispropor-tionate to their number. We as a staff contemplated the setting up of a sanctuary unit but, mainly due to a lack of enthusiasm on my part, we never did go through with the idea.

In the middle 1970s I moved to Devon to become a Senior Adviser for secondary education. Devon is not quite the idyllic educational scene one might expect. Its urban and rural areas offer contrasting styles, each with its own peculiar brand of problems. The holiday resort areas bring their own particular brand of problem to the schools. Life does, nevertheless, move at a slightly slower pace and the attitudes of the children reflect that pace. One particular urban area within the county had local govern-ment reorganization, the raising of the school leaving age and the intro-duction of a comprehensive system all in the same year. It is while a school is trying to find its identity as a comprehensive school that it can come under the critical eye of the public. Undoubtedly, this can be a traumatic time for a school but I believe that it will have discovered its true identity by the time it has become completely comprehensive. Where the change to comprehensive education is complete it seems to be the opinion that in the newly created schools the disciplinary problems are certainly not greater and may be less than the sum of the problems encountered in the separate schools prior to reorganization. I would go further than this and say that in many instances the problems are much fewer. This may be because we are now getting greater teacher stability and because teachers entering the profession have to pass through a more selective form of entry. I am reasonably optimistic about the present standard of discipline in schools although I agree that one cannot afford to be complacent. There is so much that can be done to improve the present standards even more. What can one learn from those teachers who are present in every school and who seem to have no difficulty with the children, who are respected, from whom and with whom children learn easily and well, who never seem to punish and who are dedicated to their task? Too frequently they are thought of as charismatic characters with a kind of mystique which the majority of lesser mortals will never possess. Certainly, there are teachers who teach by instinct in the same way that some fliers can be said to fly aeroplanes by 'the seat of their trousers'. Not all such instinctive teachers are necessarily good teachers and there are examples of teachers who have this kind of talent but who waste it by a form of ritual laziness. In universities, colleges and schools we must do much more to dissect the actions of the good classroom teacher and make the results available to other teachers, particularly those who are about to enter the profession.

To this end the work being done by the Teacher Education Project at the Nottingham University School of Education is most encouraging. In this project Professor Wragg and Dr Sutton have analysed many classroom incidents to see if any particular pattern of classroom interaction emerged as a result of their observations. Not surprisingly, they present personal relationships, preparation and planning of lessons, beginnings and endings of lessons and vigilance in the classroom as key issues. Since the appropriateness of the work done in the lesson is of the utmost importance, discipline cannot be regarded as something different from the learning process in the classroom. I have seen teachers in trouble because they appear to suffer from 'tunnel vision'. They appear unaware, or don't want to be aware, of the actions of children outside a particular line of vision. The ordinarily mischievous child soon learns the point of advantage in such a teacher's classroom.

Professor Wragg says that you can recognize the skilful classroom manager out shopping on a Saturday morning by the way his eyeballs roll around his head, giving him the slightly hunted look of a fugitive master spy. One is heartened by the work being done in individual schools for the probationary teacher and one is struck too by the attitude of new entrants to the profession. They appear very willing to have their lessons looked at by their colleagues, particularly if constructive and helpful comments are proffered. Similarly, they see the point of observing the

86

lessons of other teachers. More of them are now avoiding the mistake of making the over-familiar approach towards their pupils as they realistically accept that a high position in the popularity polls is not a first priority.

Children are nowadays much more critical of the ways in which teachers prepare their lessons and the concern they show for the children's work. The teacher who marks most, if not all the children's homework, and a fair proportion of classwork, and who seeks opportunities to make constructive comments about the work of his pupils, will find that the children will form a closer relationship with him. Children have not much use for teachers who think that the term is over after the end of examinations. The most boring experience one can have is to be told to get on with some of your own work for the greater part of a day. Children like to be worked hard, whether they are in rural Devon or in the inner areas of big cities, and they do not easily forgive teachers who in their opinion are not working sufficiently hard.

To maintain discipline then in the modern classroom calls for greater classroom skills on the part of the teacher. The teacher who is able to organize his classroom, teach his subject in an interesting manner, show concern for and interest in the progress of his pupils and maintain order in a firm and fair fashion will achieve the same quality of discipline in the classroom as did the teachers of twenty years ago. Despite the changes in attitude that have taken place within society there is still that same healthy respect in most ordinary homes for the good teacher. The maintenance of discipline will never quite be as easy as it was in 1935 when one of my valued ex-colleagues, at the commencement of his career in an all-age school in a textile district of Yorkshire, was able to settle his fifty-one pupils down to some work, move to an adjacent classroom, set work to the fifty-two pupils of his absent head teacher and return to his own class who would be getting on with their work without a murmur. I would not have given him the same invigilatory task in 1975, his year of retirement; such an assignment would have been regarded as counter-productive, demanding too much from the teacher's stamina. Yet, in his own classroom, he had very good standards of discipline, equally as effective as those he had achieved forty years before. As a good professional he had automatically modified his techniques with the passing of the years but the end result was remarkably unchanged.

There are, however, occasions in teaching when the maintenance of disciplinary standards makes greater demands upon the teacher than hitherto, and those are in situations which occur outside the teacher's classroom. For numerous reasons I will always be a convinced supporter of the large school, but it does make different and greater demands upon a teacher by virtue of its size. There are many more children in the school who are not taught by you and the ones you don't teach always look more threatening than the ones you do. When you are on break duty and you see an apparent lout pinning a smaller boy against a corridor wall you are not to know that they are really inseparable friends; over-reaction on your part can create an unnecessary crisis. Similar misjudgments are made by the general public who assume, genuinely or deliberately, that the actions of a small minority of pupils are indicative of the standards of the whole school. In any school, but particularly in a large school, the teacher on duty has to be vigilant when patrolling areas within the school where certain characters, left unchallenged, will turn those places into 'no go' areas for other children. These same characters are more likely to be the smokers and to commit whatever acts of vandalism are being committed in the school. I confess that I felt uplifted when, investigating six incidences of vandalism which had been committed in different parts of the school, I found that one particular child had perpetrated all six. My recurrent nightmare was that there were six different groups in action. I often wonder how much 'vandalism' in schools is really vandalism and how much can be attributed to unthinking actions on the part of pupils and inferior furnishing fittings. I once remember hitting the roof at the sight of four wash basins ripped off the wall in the fifth-form boys' toilet within one hour of the fifth form being permitted to take over their new ROSLA block. I returned to my room with my morale at a low ebb only to find one particular accident-prone lad standing outside my door ready to admit his responsibility for the damage. I don't think that he ever really understood why I shook him by the hand. Then, to an admiring audience of senior and pastoral staff, the boy demonstrated how if, foolishly, you perched yourself on the corner of the end wash basin you could set up a chain reaction which would bring down the other three wash basins from the wall. Half-inch screws were replaced by two-inch screws and that kind of 'vandalism' never occurred again.

All teachers, and particularly those on duty, have to develop antennae which will detect instances of bullying. I am certain that the actual physical bullying which took place in my boys' grammar school in the 1930s and 1940s was greater than anything which takes place in schools today, but its limits were more predictable and while none the less painful to the recipient, it was much closer to a form of ritual horseplay. Certainly, there were many more playground fights in those days than there are today. Nowadays, there is less action but, possibly, a greater fear of the unknown, particularly on the part of girls who are supposed to have either made insulting remarks about other girls or, even worse, captured the boy friend of a girl in another group. Girls, more than boys, seem to be so dependent upon the immediate friendship of another girl and are more likely to form cliques which reject other girls within the class, even if this means inventing somewhat spurious reasons for this rejection. I do not believe that male members of staff should deal solely with the problems of boys and female staff solely with the problems of girls, but a greater responsibility does fall upon the proportionately smaller number of women in a coeducational school to supervise changing-areas and toilets so that children with good attitudes can feel that their teachers care about their welfare.

The supervision of the lesson of an absent colleague is more of a chore today even when the absent teacher, as he should always try to do, leaves work set for the class. If you yourself don't teach the children, and you are less likely to in a larger school, you will not have had the opportunity to establish that special relationship with the class which only comes from previous knowledge of one another's quirks. The children may not know that you are a splendid fellow and a sound disciplinarian into the bargain. So, inevitably, some charming little member of the advanced reconnaissance patrol will do his worst. For the teacher with somewhat average classroom control, and one who takes some time to prove himself to his classes, supervision of other classes can be something of an ordeal. A perusal of the percentage absence rates of teachers can tell us a lot about the teacher and the possible stresses under which he is working. In London in the 1960s the rate of absence for reasons of sickness in the school in which I taught must have averaged around 8 to 10 per cent; in the West Riding it was about 3 per cent. If one is to make real sense of these percentages one cannot afford to neglect other important factors such as the travelling conditions to and from school and the actual time which the journey takes.

If, then, I am optimistic about the present-day standards of discipline within the classroom, and not unduly pessimistic about the situation outside the classroom, why is it that there is public concern about present-day standards? One could argue that much of this concern is misplaced but that would be evading the real question which may well be – why are there such variations in the standards achieved by schools? Why do children in some schools feel happier and more secure than children who go to schools in what would be regarded as more favourable areas?

I know that the quality of the leadership exercised by the head teacher is of the utmost importance, and we all have a particular charismatic character in mind when we use that phrase. I believe however that there is an insufficient recognition of the contribution which a dedicated body of teachers can make to creating the right ethos within a school, apart from the leadership qualities of the head. Regrettably, all teachers are not agreed upon the means by which one makes the school into a friendly and caring community and there is a reluctance on the part of some to take calculated risks. Some teachers, frustrated in their ambitions by what they see as a head with intransigent attitudes, indulge in an internecine warfare with him to the disadvantage of both school and children. What are the means by which a school can strive to show itself to be friendly and caring?

The class teacher should be made the bulwark of the system. The young teachers in particular wish to fill this role in a positive and creative way. Children should be allowed access to the building and to their classrooms at all times. It should not be beyond the wit of man to make laboratories safe at the time when they are not being used for lessons. In return, we should demand of the children that they exercise a sense of responsibility and a fair amount of self-discipline. Teachers who undertake a share of supervisory duties at lunch time do much to ensure that the children in their care are protected from fear. Dinner-ladies, for all their virtues, cannot adequately provide this protection in a secondary school. We must take renewed pride in that particularly British phenomenon, the out-of-school activity, which draws pupils and staff together in close association. Fifth and sixth forms usually have their own social areas – why not social areas for fourth-, and even third-, formers? Year councils with pupils exercising real supervisory function over matters of immediate concern to them are more realistic than pseudo-democratic school councils. Form or tutor groups should be mixed in ability. The system under which teaching groups are organized should take cognizance of this fact. The appropriateness of the content of the curriculum for every pupil should be reappraised from time to time. Some part of the fourth- and fifth-form curriculum should be devoted to preparing the youngsters for subsequent stages in their lives. The sanctions of a school should be made clear and explicit. There appears to be no place for corporal punishment as one of those sanctions.

Finally, what can parents and the community in the immediate vicinity of the school do to help? It makes good sense, where it is feasible, for a school to become a community college. It is my impression that in Devon, the facilities in community schools are better cared for than is the norm, despite the fact that the premises are more frequently used. Where schools have shared resources with the community there have been encouraging reports of success. The attendance of adults at examination classes in school time seems to have had beneficial effects. Children are more likely to see the relevance of a school which develops such links with the community. What help can the school receive to enable it to deal more effectively with the inevitable and usually small minority of badly behaved children who, despite the caring nature of the school, disrupt the work of others? For them, is it to be suspension, 'isolation' or a sanctuary unit? Or are there other resources within our communities, human and material, which can be used to help schools deal with what may be the fundamental discipline problem facing schools today?

10 Discipline: a search for meaning

Sister Marie Philippa
Head of Notre Dame School, Sheffield

Each morning at 9.00 a.m. I went from my office to the hall, where about three hundred girls of a year-group, and about twelve members of staff stood in silence, awaiting my arrival. The morning assembly had begun. Sometimes I conducted assembly, at other times a member of staff, or a group of class from the year; in all cases, the assembled girls listened politely and participated with three hundred varying degrees of attention and enthusiasm. The ceremony was carried out each morning for a different year-group in an orderly and dignified manner, in an atmosphere that was relaxed, good-humoured and responsive. At no time did any girl call out, cause a disturbance, start a muttering or a giggling campaign, or engage in any activity which could be considered disruptive. I have often wondered why this does not happen, why three hundred girls accept the discipline such a large gathering imposes. It is not because the conformists and the peaceable arrive early and the troublesome arrive late; the latecomers are as varied as the assembly group, and when they do arrive, they appear to listen, or at least remain quiet. This pattern of good order continues for the most part, on the corridors and in the classrooms, so that the overall impression is one of quiet and good order, and between lessons, of an orderly flow of traffic along the corridors. This is the normal situation we take for granted in school, although disruption and disorder of different kinds by an individual or a group do occur, but because we have high standards of acceptable behaviour, such instances are attended to immediately as a means of returning to the norm. On the other hand, it is interesting to note the preconceived notions of visitors to a large comprehensive school in an area of multiple social and economic disadvantage, which has received such a poor image in the press and on television. They arrive, expecting to see and hear noisy, yelling pupils in outlandish clothes, hurling abuse at one another, giving cheek to staff, lounging about, doing no work, or rushing headlong down corridors so that visitors have to take cover or flatten themselves against the wall for fear of being knocked down in the rush. They are surprised when none of these things occur; instead, they remark on the quiet, the order, the work being done in class, the neat appearance of the girls in uniform, and their friendly attitude when they are taken to different parts of the campus, and the girls 'chat them up' on the way. It is true they will see some loungers, latecomers and lazy pupils, but that is the pattern in most schools.

Because of their surprised reaction to the reality of the school, I have, once I have recovered from my indignation at their sometimes condescending comments, thought about the quality of life in the school as it concerns conduct, attitudes, control, in effect, *discipline*. If a school has a reputation for good discipline, or is a place with no discipline, what does it mean? Is discipline an end in itself, something to be obtained at all costs, or does it lead to something else? What is discipline for the schools of the late 1970s?

The word *discipline* has undergone some linguistic changes, yet basically the meaning is the same as always, and has to do with the *discipuli* – those in the learning situation, who are placed in the care of a competent qualified person, with the authority to bring about conditions which enable learning to take place. This learning is concerned not only with acquiring knowledge of a trade or profession, but with learning to become a whole person. Because of the need for control by recognized authority, discipline has acquired the additional meaning of being associated with well-drilled good order, imposed by authority, carrying with it the notion of sanctions for violation of the code of rules. Our idea of discipline depends to a great extent on our concept of the nature of man and of the child in particular. If we see man as inherently evil, but capable of improvement by means of stern methods during his early years, the methods used will be harsh and repressive, based on the maxim of 'spare the rod and spoil the child'. This applied more to the methods used in schools of the nineteenth and early twentieth century, and are unlikely to be used much today. However, one wonders if this is the view of those who still accept the use of corporal punishment in schools. There is also the view based on the philosophy of man's innate goodness and freedom, that training and education are based on the principle of freedom from all restraint and the exaltation of self-assertion and self-expression. If we believe, however, that man is a developing creature, capable of good and evil, worthy of respect, with the capacity to fulfil himself and work for others, discipline will be regarded as a means of giving the opportunities to develop individual qualities, to restrain evil tendencies and to live as a member of society, conscious of a life beyond the boundaries of one's own existence. The individual requires conditions which give scope for the development of the personality, not only by the assimilation of knowledge, but also by active and enjoyable participation in the process of learning, alone, and with others.

As I consider this third view of the nature of man to be valid, it forms the basis for the aims and objectives I have for a school, which in turn determine my views on discipline. Some years ago I presented the following to the staff for their consideration:

Aims
The development of every girl as a fully human person, in a Christian way of life.

Objectives

1 To provide the environment of a Catholic community, living according to the gospel, in which every girl can be helped to become fully human, and to be aware of her responsibilities in helping others in the community, the home, the school, the Church and society to become fully human.

2 To use all available resources and services in developing the potential of every girl so that her physical, intellectual, emotional, social, moral, spiritual and cultural education leads to the formation of a mature Christian woman, conscious of her own worth and dignity.

3 To provide in the curriculum courses which give every girl the opportunity to be extended to her full capabilities so that she becomes a well-balanced, integrated person, aware of the world about her, and the world beyond her neighbourhood.

4 To help the girls realize that education is a continuous process, and therefore they need to acquire skills and attitudes which will prepare them to live fully in a constantly changing society.

This was accepted as the groundwork for the aspects we considered essential in the organization of a school, and discipline is about all of these things: academic and pastoral structure, the curriculum, the physical conditions, the network of relationships and the interaction of head, staff, pupils, and the many groups connected with the school.

The organization of the school has to be structured in such a way that staff and pupils have a stable framework in which to operate; its validity and effectiveness will be tested by the way in which it allows for the development of good relationships, gives scope for initiative, and has sufficient flexibility to enable change to take place, without leaving anyone in a state of uncertainty. Interest and concern for the person within the community of the school is paramount, and it matters little whether vertical house-groups or year-groups form the basis of the pastoral structure; what matters is how the system works for the benefit of the pupils. In the same way, the academic organization, while taking note of educational developments nationally, must reflect the way in which an individual school meets the needs of its pupils, so that there are elements which work well in one school but would not be required in another. Such a feature is the general studies department which is concerned with the pastoral, academic and curricular needs of less able fourth- and fifth-year girls. Because of its special organization it has a certain measure of success by providing a curriculum in a pastoral setting which is relevant to the world of these girls. Its effectiveness can be judged by the fact that there are few instances of disruptive behaviour which cannot be remedied within the department itself. If the organization exists so that learning takes place, the compilation of the school timetable, which is, in effect, the application of curriculum structure and content in the day-today working situation, is all important. It has to be planned well in advance and carefully thought out, both in the deployment of staff and resources, and in a consideration of the educational development of the pupils. No timetable will ever be perfect; it is impossible to satisfy everyone, because of the constraints placed on the timetabler by the available accommodation, staffing, time, and resources, but a timetable completed on the basis of expediency, the self-interest of the strongest members of staff, inadequate forward planning, or what is more likely, on the unchanging pattern used by the timetabler for years, without reappraisal each year, is likely to lead to dissatisfaction among staff and pupils and their parents. A timetable which reflects and puts into practice the objectives of the school, whatever its shortcomings, provides a secure framework in which to operate, and is the gateway to good order. It is one thing, however, to have a competent timetable, with all lessons accounted for so that we can speak knowingly about balanced curriculum etc. but when it comes to curriculum content in relation to discipline, we are concerned with what is actually taught in the classroom or workshop. The curriculum offered has to be such that it challenges all the pupils in the learning situation, being neither too weak to be demanding, nor too strong to be discouraging. It has to motivate learning, and help the pupils apply themselves to the task in hand. We are concerned, therefore, with a curriculum which is relevant and suitable, gives scope for individualized learning and group activity, provides opportunity for the exercise of initiative and responsibility, and the freedom to develop as an individual person, accepting at the same time that such development takes place in a community situation, and usually in a particular geographical location within a building we call school.

If our task is to create conditions for learning, we have to consider the physical conditions in which we work, and the resources available to us. In planning school buildings, it would appear that architects have given little thought to the importance of features which help in maintaining order as well as providing a safe environment: space for ease of movement on corridors and staircases, rooms which are comfortable, visually pleasing, reasonably soundproof, and adequately heated, with sufficient light and ventilation. A building which generates noise by echoing and carrying sound, corridors which are congested when pupils move from one room to another, uncomfortable rooms, are all features which make order difficult to maintain. So it is the task of the head and senior staff to examine the impact of the physical conditions on staff and pupils, and to find ways of providing for safety and order, and comfort, despite deficiencies and limitations. It means involving everyone in the task of ensuring that corridors, rooms and surroundings are clean, tidy and attractive. This is why we try to find solutions to the litter problem, why we eliminate as quickly as possible any deliberate or inadvertent scrawling on walls. By inculcating a respect for the appearance of the building and

94

its contents, staff and pupils are given the responsibility of helping each other to enjoy and utilize the resources and amenities provided.

This attitude is possible only if there is involvement, and the extent of the involvement depends on the quality of the relationships within the school. It is possible to have a school so highly organized that it is like an efficient machine where everyone has to fit into the system; it is also possible to have a school which is like 'one big happy family'; one is efficient, impersonal; the other is disorganized, haphazard, probably full of personal warmth, but unlikely to survive the rigours of the demands of education today. Planning and organization are essential, but our planning is for the sake of people, so as to make the forming of relationships possible in the learning situation; discipline forms part of the process of interaction among pupils and staff. This is at its most practical at classroom level, and the individual teachers are concerned about what happens between them and the pupils they teach. Some of us probably have a secret nightmare in which the class is completely out of our control so that we become victims of defiance, jeering, derision. In fact, in the general run of schools, this extreme rarely occurs. When it does there are many factors involved. Recently, the press and television gave a great deal of publicity to outbreaks of unruly behaviour by pupils in some schools, when teachers withdrew their services of supervision during the lunch hour. Most of us were no doubt relieved that it did not happen in our own school, and we were also, I should think, angry at the highlighting of such incidents, when most schools continued to function in their normal manner, even if there were problems. Pupils on the rampage in a school make headline news at any time; society, as a rule, is surprised, shocked; schools are criticised for their poor management, incompetent teachers and so on. But violence at football grounds on Saturdays, violence and struggles between rival factions at demonstrations on Sundays, not to mention violence during industrial disputes, shown at its worst in the Grunwick affair, have almost become part of a way of life in our society. It is rare to find responsibility for such activities ascribed to anyone; no one is blamed, except, perhaps, once more, the schools for not producing quiet, obedient, conforming, law-abiding citizens. I once made the comment that 'society gets the schools it deserves', but I consider that today, society gets better schools than it deserves. The question to ask is not, why is there serious unruly behaviour in our schools, but rather, why is there so little of such activity, considering that our pupils live in a world where lawful authority at all levels is challenged, questioned and flouted? Schools are expected to run counter to the evils and disturbances in society, and to reflect all that is good and worthwhile, with little or no support from society. Again, I ask, why is it that, generally speaking, our schools are places of good order, where learning does take place, albeit reluctantly, by some pupils, yet the adults with the authority to do this are outnumbered by the pupils at a ratio of approximately 17:1 in the secondary sector?

The answer to this question is to be found in the attitudes of the pupils, as much as in the conditions created by head and staff. Their reasons for cooperating with the figures of authority in the school, for observing the patterns of discipline, are complex. There is the need to be accepted as a member of the school community, particularly at class grouping level, and so pupils usually conform to the organized practices and traditions. There is the fear of the consequences of breaking the code, either in being sanctioned or punished in some way by authority, or of being singled out as different. There is the desire to please, to be well thought of. All these are motives for cooperation, but I think there is another reason; the pupils themselves want an orderly, secure, stable and happy environment, and they look to those in authority to provide it. Chaos and disorder exhaust people's energy; giving the pupils complete freedom of choice as a means of covering up our own indecision, uncertainty and laziness leads to boredom, frustration, disruption, damage to property, and ultimately to the destruction of people as individuals, because it destroys true freedom and responsibility and the opportunity to form worthwhile relationships. Pupils want to know what they have to do, where they should go, and will therefore cooperate with us in ensuring an orderly situation in which they feel sufficiently secure and relaxed to learn, to develop, and, on occasion, to risk having a brush with authority, to see how far they can go. The head and the staff in this case are the enablers and facilitators who make possible the conditions in which this cooperation leads to the forming of good relationships between staff and pupils.

A teacher should be able to encounter a class of upwards of thirty pupils, either for the first time or for the forty-first time, secure in the knowledge that head and staff generally hold the same views and adopt the same policy about the constituents of order and discipline in a particular school. It is a help to staff if there is open acknowledgement of problems and difficulties which have to be faced, and that they will receive support when the need arises. The school in turn expects the teacher to be professionally competent, not only in what is taught, but more important – *who* is taught. There is a world of difference between teaching mathematics to IIIA and teaching IIIA mathematics. It is perhaps a sweeping generalization to state that anyone with specialized knowledge can teach their subject, especially to bright pupils; but it is a fact that *teaching people* requires gifts over and above the possession of specialized knowledge. Within the classroom problems of disorder or lack of motivation to learning occur because the needs of the particular pupils are not being considered. Every teacher, and not just the head, has to lead, and so requires certain qualities of leadership: the art of foreseeing and forestalling and the gift requested by Solomon – a discerning heart and mind. Foreseeing includes all that we associate with planning, preparation, reflection on the personality of the individual pupil, and on the group personality as well; forestalling is concerned with all the devices we use to eliminate any trouble which might arise, and not waiting until it happens and then deciding what to do. Both require awareness, sensitivity to people and situations, commonsense, a sense of humour, and the capacity to be unsurprised by the unexpected. Good relationships are established when the pupils see there is consistency of approach and method, fair play, concern for them as individuals and that the teacher has the ability to relax with them, to laugh with them and not at them. There is a need to acquire the quality of discerning when to act, when to keep one eye closed, and, on occasion, to keep both eyes closed; of not taking every infraction of rule or act of disobedience as a personal affront. The mood of the class has to be constantly tested, and discernment is required, for example, in our method of approach to 2B at second lesson on a Tuesday, and the same class, during the last lesson on Friday afternoon. Discipline is linked to motivation, to interest, to helping the pupils think for themselves, and take responsibility for their own learning, but sometimes teacher and pupil can acquiesce in a debilitating situation where little learning occurs. Pupils often want others to do their thinking for them, to tell them things they should know; they tend to cause trouble when given an assignment which challenges, and which does not give the 'instant' results they have learned to expect from watching TV Quiz Programmes. They are happy writing and copying large blocks of information from books, because it does not require the effort of thinking, and yet gives the impression of work being done. For the sake of peace and quiet at any price, some teachers resort to these methods, so that both parties are lulled into a situation of thinking this is learning. It becomes all the more difficult, therefore, for the teacher who wants pupils to think, who tries to wean them away from the security of dictated notes so that the classroom becomes a battleground of wills, between the teacher concerned to educate, and pupils who do not wish to be challenged to think. There is no easy answer to this, but given the good relationship between teacher and pupil, the real business of learning can be accomplished.

These reflections on discipline might give the impression that I am unaware of the problems of disorder and disruption that occur in schools. This is not so, but it is necessary to discuss the bases of discipline in a school, before looking at the issue of indiscipline, particularly in the classroom. Given that the school management has done everything to provide satisfactory conditions for learning, why should some classes be disorderly and the teachers exhausted in the struggle to maintain order? Generally, the disruption, the defiance, the refusal to cooperate by a group of pupils, does not affect all the staff who teach them. If this is the case, the cause is likely to be in the staff member – inexperienced in dealing with people, lacking in sensitivity, unimaginative, ingenuous or naive, lessons inadequately prepared, the list could go on, and might include just being utterly incompetent and ineffectual. So what is to be done in such a situation? First, there has to be support from within the school, in the form of advice from more experienced colleagues, in having a system whereby a teacher obtains help immediately from heads of departments and other senior staff. Where a departmental staff is located together in a building, often the disruptive pupil can be removed for a 'cooling-off' period, so that the lesson may continue with fewer interruptions. Second, the teacher has to undertake a self-appraisal of attitudes, methods, strengths, weaknesses, and in the light of this, work out the remedies suitable for the occasion. But what help can be given to the ineffectual and incompetent teacher who is unable to control any class sufficiently for the pupils to learn? We have to consider the situation of the teacher as a person who could be destroyed by the experience, but there are the pupils who must be protected from the effects of poor teaching, as a matter of justice. The teaching profession as a whole has not yet solved this problem and the school can only continue to support the teacher, and nullify as far as possible the detrimental effect on the school until such time as the teacher recognizes the futility of remaining in the profession.

When we come to a consideration of the disruptive or disaffected individual or group, the position is rather different. The pupils may be so because the curriculum is irrelevant, school may be irrelevant to their real life; it may be due to serious problems in the home and the family, or there can be a range of social and economic factors causing frustration and anger which shows itself in defiance and unruly conduct in school, with the teacher used as the escape valve for pent-up emotions. If a teacher has to face disruption of this kind, there must be support and help; it is small comfort to be told that home conditions are the cause, and that the pupil requires sympathy, understanding, encouragement. No one will be more understanding of the problems than a dedicated teacher, but when twenty-five other pupils have to be taught, the question of priorities is important: who comes first, the twenty-five who want to learn or the one or two who don't? The individual and special care needed requires the use of the support services of the education authority, in addition to the parents who have to be totally involved in the problem. Parental involvement in, and knowledge of, their children's conduct in school is one of the most effective ways of dealing with problems of indiscipline. If a pupil knows that the school policy in matters of serious breaches of school rules is to inform the parents and request their presence at the school, the climb-down from the defiant challenging attitude to teachers or the bullying, threatening approach to other pupils, is very marked. Many of the day-to-day infringements, the minor incidents, which are a nuisance and cause inconvenience, can be dealt with on the spot, but persistent bad behaviour requires other measures. Again, the cooperation of the parents means that the pupil is subject to two sets of pressures, and a weekly report on attendance in the case of truancy, or attitude in class, or homework, can bring about an improvement, if for no other reason than to be rid of the inconvenience of having the teacher of every lesson sign the report. The follow-up is as important as the initial exercise, and if parents come to school frequently to know what is happening, the situation does improve.

The school is only one of many organizations involved in the task of transforming pupils into adults, and our particular function is to accomplish this by instruction, by training, by developing a self-discipline which encourages initiative and enterprise and acts against adopting the easy way out of difficulties and the demand for instant satisfaction. We are here to educate the reason, emotion, will, so that vision, passion, commitment will lead to the discovery of the reality contained in the search for truth, beauty and the power of goodness.

11 A parent's view

Elizabeth Wallis

As a parent and the only 'spectator' among the contributors to this book – and perhaps one who sees more of the game – I have come to believe that what society desires from the child is not to be educated in the true sense of the word, but to conform. And conformity above all with a rigid examination system which at best will ensure the failure of the majority. Furthermore, I see that many of the education institutions do the job badly and create more problems than they solve.

In support of these ideas and as some explanation as to why I hold them I should like to draw on my personal experience.

I was born in a London suburb of a Methodist father and an Italian Catholic mother. My father, who now appears to me to have been very Victorian in his outlook, had been an RSM in the army and my mother was the daughter of an Italian officer in the Egyptian police. But although my father was more affected by religion than my mother (I would not have called either of them religious), I was sent to a Catholic primary school.

In retrospect I realize the school was mostly attended by the sons and daughters of poor Irish immigrants. It was a one-storey depressed-looking brick building in a small asphalt area divided into two halves for play, one for the boys and one for the girls. There were only four class-rooms with a cloakroom at one end and the headmistress's room at the other, with a corridor running down one side. We had very little equipment. In fact I don't remember any except a few bound books, exercise books, pencils and blackboards. Most of the teachers were nuns and the one in charge was terrifying, as was the teacher in the fourth year.

The discipline was absolute and none of us, whatever our intelligence, had any doubt as to what was expected of us. We had a card to fill in every Monday morning asking us if we had been to church, to Holy Communion, to Confession and to Sunday School, in that order, and heaven help the one who put a cross instead of a tick. We also learnt the Catechism off by heart and said it daily. But in all my childhood I never recall being formally punished by my parents or my teachers.

I suppose I must have learnt a lot more than I thought there, because although I didn't relate to any of the pupils except another girl like myself who lived in quite a smart road, as I did, I won a scholarship with an enormous choice of schools attached to it. My father, though somewhat anti-semitic (which was then fashionable), decided to send me to a Jewish school in Hampstead, because he said Jews always worked hard at school and knew how to get on in the world. Convents, on the other hand, didn't appear to teach anything very much except how to sew. I realize now that this decision might have been made because my brother had won a scholarship from the same Catholic primary school to a Catholic day boys' public school and his school career had been a total disaster, as he refused to conform to the rigid and sometimes violent discipline. He was once flogged (their word) in front of the whole school as an alternative to expulsion, for being indiscriminating enough to fight the son of an Inspector of Schools on a railway station. This experience could have had something to do with his subsequent lack of progress.

However, I was only at the Jewish school for a couple of years as the family moved and I was sent to a girls' grammar school, where religion was taught much as I would imagine it is today, ineffectively, even though the somewhat formidable headmistress used to teach it.

By this time I began to hate school. I found it dull, boring and without meaning. Nevertheless, I matriculated well and went into the sixth form as was expected of somebody of my academic ability but left in the middle of the first year as I felt I was suffocating.

My interest in formal education ceased from that day until my sons were due to start primary school. I then started thinking about it again. As a child I was a great reader and most of my reading took the form of school stories – mainly those set in boys' boarding schools. I think *Tom Brown's Schooldays* was my favourite book at the time. I longed to go to a school that I could feel totally committed to and where there was a complete self-supporting community.

Unfortunately, the nearest school to our house was a church school. Like all lapsed Catholics I didn't really think the Protestant Church was a serious religion because it didn't invoke hell and eternal damnation, and have gradations of sin from mortal to venial. My husband had had no religion in his upbringing at all, so he was as disturbed as I was by the attempted indoctrination supported by a form of discipline which we didn't at first appreciate. The outcome has been that both my sons appear to be actively hostile to organized religion and view the whole subject with boredom or even blasphemy.

My elder son became very upset by the violent behaviour of a male teacher in the third year of the primary school. Although this teacher never once struck him, his attitude to other children terrified my son, who began to have sleepless nights, and I was forced to move him to a state school somewhat further from our home. I also removed my younger son and I am eternally grateful that I did.

My elder son, now seventeen and at a sixth-form college, has never had any more discipline problems at school, even though he has come up against teachers who were not above giving a quick cuff, but were not ritually cruel or callous. The coeducational school I sent him to after the

Church school was very relaxed. The headmaster did not believe in, nor practise, corporal punishment, even though the local authority sanctioned it. I learnt from attending council education committee meetings that the prevailing Tory councillors were only too happy to respond to the teachers' organizations' demands that corporal punishment should be retained for boys between seven and sixteen, though not for girls at all. My sons always complain about this sexual discrimination although neither has ever been caned.

At the primary school to which I removed my sons, the headmaster, a humorous and outspoken character, used to say he didn't need the cane to keep order, which was quite true as he had a marvellous personality.

The boys soon discovered that the new head who replaced him did not have the same views on the cane. One persistently naughty boy came out of his room one day bleeding. He told all his friends he had been caned on the legs. Later it was found to be quite untrue. He had waited in the room and nobody came so he had covered his legs with blood from a loose tooth – one of the unforeseen consequences of permitting corporal punishment, perhaps.

I have come to believe very strongly in the state system of education as a matter of principle and feel we should all fight to make it better. But I now realize that an education system such as ours will never really improve quickly until we rid ourselves of the class divisions which have the damaging consequences of too high a proportion of the population undervaluing themselves; a lack of confidence which can be reinforced by authoritarian attitudes.

All too rarely do we consider the basic rights of children. As society becomes more and more organized and the administration of government penetrates more and more into every area of our lives, it becomes more apparent that, as Ethel Mannin wrote in 1931 in *Commonsense and the Child*:

> Parents, nurses and teachers are natural enemies of the child because they are the destroyers of children's freedom. They represent authority from the beginning and children's liberty is interfered with the moment they are born.

Thus I question not only the teacher's role but also that of the parent. It is true that parents are free to send a child away from home to a boarding school (a peculiarly British phenomenon this) or not to send the child to school at all if they can prove they are capable of educating him at home. But it is mandatory for children between the ages of five and sixteen to spend five days a week, seven hours a day and forty weeks a year in an educational establishment and thus compulsorily removed from the parent.

There is little consultation or cooperation between the school and the home despite the research by J. W. B. Douglas and G. W. Miller in the early 1970s which showed that a main factor in pupil attainment is the encouragement and interest of parents. Parents are for the most part instructed, if informed at all, in the ways of the school – punctuality, uniform, homework, reasons for absence, but they are usually only told the absolute minimum. Sometimes opportunities are given for questions, but it is very difficult for parents to express themselves properly at meetings, when the memories of their schooldays flood back and their fear of the system reasserts itself.

It is amazing how complete the conditioning is and how it can be measured by the parents who never show up at school and want no part in the education of their children.

When publicly asked to defend their approach to discipline, teachers make play of *in loco parentis* to justify any form of it, especially corporal punishment. Is it not an affront to the freedom of the parent, but more especially to the child, when a teacher has the backing of the law to impose discipline without consulting the parent? Accountability is too often rejected on the grounds that the professional is the best person to decide. Many LEAs have no rules governing discipline in schools and too many boards of managers and governors do not exercise the powers they possess in law because they have not been informed about them.

As the American writer William Kvaraceus wrote in 1971:

As they first enter school, most children – rich or poor, black or white – are immediately absorbed into a massive educational system; they enter school only on the school's terms and on the basis of unconditional surrender. These terms often demand renunciation of self and constant submission to processes of conformity and standardization. Most schools achieve their goals at the price to the individual of some loss of privacy, personal identity and individuality. They require at least our conformity to external authority and subservience to the strong pressures of the peer group. They invoke the severe competitive processes of selection and survival of the academically fit. All too frequently they provide an artificial separation between the classroom and the life stream of everyday problems and issues.

Those who are unable or unwilling to submit to the social system frequently join the ranks of the failures, the troubled and the troublesome, the dropouts and the delinquents or, in defence, they may set up their own ego-supporting institutions in the form of the underground press, the delinquent gang, or the anti-establishment political party.

So teachers are caught in a trap. If the law demands the attendance of every child, then the teacher has to accept every child. Too often they must cope with too many children at once, in inadequate buildings with too few resources and with a confusion of messages coming through from the 'real' world as to what they are supposed to be communicating to their pupils. The wonder is that there are not more disciplinary problems, but it must be, as David Williams said in *A Treatise on Education in 1774*: 'The disposition to knowledge is as natural to the mind, as the desire of food is to the body.'

Children want to learn and need to learn, but not necessarily what the curriculum and the fashions of the time dictate. As Williams went on to say: 'When the taste [for learning] is vitiated, we must have recourse to expedients; and among those that offer themselves, choose the least injurious.'

Of course, many schools respect the children and their individuality and do attempt to achieve results, i.e. examination passes without crippling the essential creativity of the individual child. One of the advantages of mixed-ability teaching is that discipline problems are reduced and the needs of the individual child are taken seriously. But unfortunately our society only appears to value what can be measured in the narrowest terms. The result is that only a small percentage pass and the great majority must therefore be seen to fail. Living with failure in the school community as the majority of pupils do must add to disciplinary problems.

David Williams also observed in *A Treatise on Education*:

A boy whose object is to be advancement, and not virtue, should be educated in the established schools of every community. The reason is not so much for the connections he may make, or the celebrity he may acquire, as that his very soul will be moulded to the times, and he will come into the world perfectly fitted for it. In this view of things, education is the art of forming a citizen upon the principles and views of any particular government. His sentiments; his conscience; his mind, must be regulated by the laws of this institution; and nature must be warped by authority.

Thus one observes that discipline increases and is imposed in proportion to the degree to which a particular philosophy or ideology has to be implanted and to the importance placed on passing particular exams. The more fanatical, inadequate or neurotic the adherence to the belief, the more repressive the accompanying discipline.

Non-conformists may act from many different motives – a disturbed or poverty-stricken family background, lack of intelligence, too much intelligence, an undetected physical or mental handicap, or even natural high spirits. But it is surely important to know why bad behaviour occurs. A blanket set of punishments are obviously not effective for all misdemeanours. But what time has the hard-pressed teacher to consult parents and all the back-up services to ensure that the punishment fits the 'crime'?

Non-conformity may also result, however, from a healthy desire to preserve individuality and original creativity. When George Gershwin went to Ravel for music lessons, Ravel listened to him and said: 'Go away, I cannot teach you anything.' How does one account for the accomplishments of the self-taught, like Edison or Sean O'Casey? Perhaps a society which demands conformity to a curriculum surrounded by over-strict discipline results in apathy, uncooperativeness and lack of enthusiasm even in its apparently successful products.

Why do teachers need a framework of discipline in order to carry out their instruction if children naturally want to learn? Independent teaching methods, where the pupils take greater responsibility for their learning, have proved successful, especially if accompanied by a withdrawal system where pupils with difficulties are coached not only by teachers, but by older pupils as well.

Is discipline required because so many children are damaged by their parents by the time they arrive at school and so many others have their enthusiasm destroyed by the curriculum and teaching methods employed? It follows, then, that punishment may possibly reduce the disruptive elements and permit the motivated and the conforming to learn. But society may pay a very high price in terms of crime and neurosis if it fails to attend to its misfits and its alienated. Discipline is all too often the easy way out, the resort of a primitive being, a substitute for a proper examination of the causes of disobedience. Perhaps those damaged by over-disciplining in the older generation are those who inflict most damage on the present one. I shudder at what I hear of the thoughtless discipline in institutions for delinquents and even more for the physically and mentally handicapped.

The interesting and enthusiastic teacher seldom appears to need punishment aids. But what of the teacher who lacks character, knowledge or even real interest in the subject? If teachers are allowed to report on their children, why shouldn't children be permitted to comment on their teachers? The uninterested teacher attempting to inform the unmotivated pupil is surely a recipe for pandemonium. But to say that teachers never fail, only pupils, seems to be a heresy. When will the teachers' unions begin to be concerned about standards of competence for their members and leadership qualities in head teachers? Would a contractual relationship between teachers and authorities, and especially for head teachers, improve matters? All the in-service training in the world is not going to make some teachers better and no teacher can be taught how to like and respect children.

As a parent living in the real world and not having the money to send my child to Bedales or Summerhill where I can buy an atmosphere of freedom, concern and opportunity for my child, I must settle for the state system, with all its faults. But I think these faults could be reduced if bureaucrats were less arrogant, if teachers were more humble and parents were given a real role to play. The fact that somebody else's child doesn't want to learn and mine does affects my child's future. The bleak future of the unmotivated child must also be my concern and I would strongly question whether mere punishment can effect a change of attitude.

Perhaps a school–parent–teacher–pupil council could be created concerned with the whole life of the school – what is taught, why it is taught, how it is taught and the social framework to make it effective. I am quite sure the disciplinary situation in an egalitarian age can only be improved by treating all parties to education as equals and bringing schools more and more into the community.

Real democracy breeds maturity and self-discipline. Can society progress without these attributes and all children be valued for their intelligence and talents, however small? As long as one group feels they have an inherent right to dominate another, resentment, apathy and violence must persist. Only through democratic relationships can the handicaps from which so many children suffer – parental abuse, both mental and physical, poverty, poor housing, family breakdown, physical confinement, media propaganda and commercial exploitation – be taken into account and progress made towards their elimination.

A frightening aspect is the way the most pathetic revolt on the part of a small group is sensationalized by a media, hungry for headlines and over-simplified for an apparently uncaring readership. The causes never appear to be a matter of concern. Such reporting makes it easier for hangers and floggers to retain that cruel world in which every problem is disposed of by legalized violence of varying degrees.

Now that there is modern technology to command even greater conformity, the dangers to individual freedom and especially to children are even greater. Secrecy in record-keeping is almost equated with the defence of the realm. The use of computer records, psychiatry for the child who is 'different' and drugs for the hyperactive are becoming commonplace.

As we can no longer call upon religion and the doctrine of original sin to justify harsh measures in exacting obedience, we now use the economic weapon. But the prizes are fewer and will go only to those who pass the exams controlled by the privileged in society. Wasting time at school by the no-hopers must not be allowed to affect the chances of the children of the ambitious, so the system must be arranged accordingly. But most of those who make the rules hide their eyes from the piercing light of twentieth-century knowledge and use teachers too often as policemen for young minds, to restrict and confine them.

Well may they wonder when the brightest and the bravest, the most individual and the most damaged disobey!

12 Discipline in the primary sector

Anne Webb
Deputy head, Fields End JMI School, Hemel Hempstead

There must be many schools which aspire to be, and are in fact, 'caring' institutions. Certainly most primary schools with which I have had contact over the last ten years aim to be more than efficient academic establishments and are responsive to public demands that social and moral education require a place within the curriculum, even though there are several expressed doubts about their priority in relation to more traditional areas. There are, however, implications in the curriculum and teaching methods of a school which will often determine the nature of its social control.

At my own school the staff place a high value on independence and initiative in the learning process and consequently it would be inappropriate and counter-productive not to encourage the development of these characteristics in the social behaviour of the children. Similarly, the approbation given to sympathetic attitudes from children towards others also needs to be seen in a general tolerance and understanding of intellectual differences. An awareness of status plays a remarkably small part in methods of social control, we are a small enough establishment for this to be possible and it makes the question of discipline more personal to the child and the teacher, and more immediately relevant to the situation. It would be true to say that we do not face the harshest disciplinary problems but because we are accountable to the community for our performance in the field of social and moral education we must constantly appraise the validity of our objectives in relation to the actual behaviour of the children and the preferences of their parents.

It is inevitable that the value system of a school will not comprehensively reflect the moral codes of every parent. Notions such as honesty, obedience and loyalty may form the backbone of several such codes, but the practical interpretations will differ from home to home and therefore from child to child. When I speak to parents about encouraging a child to think for himself I may receive initial endorsement only to discover later that this conflicts with deep-rooted attitudes to loyalty developed at home and all-powerful in the school environment. When staff discuss the kind of behaviour that they would like to encourage or to discourage we try to keep the positive demonstrations of these different codes in mind recognizing that by virtue of our status as teachers, our influence will not be great, that it is the nature of our ideas that will be tested.

Honesty is not going to be an accepted norm simply because it is a cornerstone in the school philosophy. Explanation, discussion, assessment and revision will heighten the general awareness of this virtue and we aim to subject the most prominent features of the school's social and moral aims to this analysis with the children, but when that is said we must acknowledge that a facility with the language of morality does not presuppose a parallel attitude towards moral behaviour.

When a mother brings her young child to the nursery she, like the teacher, is anxious that he should be happy, that he should not grieve over-much at her absence from the scene and that he should wish to return regularly. In order for all this to be achieved he will need to make sound relationships with his peers and the adults who will work with him. For many children the social demands are met with increasing confidence and the dialogue between staff and parents helps to develop some consistency in adult responses to varying types of behaviour, a consistency that is vital if we are to achieve a moral sense of what is right, as well as a practical awareness of what is unacceptable. If it is right to be kind to friends because people deserve to be treated with kindness, then punching and pushing are wrong even if an adult is not present to stop such actions. Of course such a moral attitude is not firmly established for many years, but every effort is made to build the foundations on which a child stands when faced with individuals, situations, or questions which are not to his liking. By talking about alternatives, the effects of behaviour, and how people 'feel' when treated with kindness or otherwise, we introduce the concept of choice, that an eye for an eye is not the only, nor even the best, response although peer-group standards usually state the opposite. The 'punishment' that children expect to follow discovered 'naughtiness' cannot take the place of discussion but we sometimes feel that it has a useful role to play in an overall disciplinary strategy. The deterrent value of punishment for young children is low simply because their memories are short, and the true nature of cause and effect is obscure for them.

We have two sets of rules, both unwritten, and made publicly explicit at irregular intervals. The first set concerns the physical operation of the school, the organization of people in and around the building and is common to most schools. When children break these rules they do so not because they are unaware of the rule or disagree with it but because it imposes a restriction on their behaviour which does not suit them at some time or other. It is easier to disregard the rule than pay attention to it – and not always from the child's point of view alone! It can be that a learning activity must be disrupted if a teacher is to respond to the breaking of one of these 'physical' rules, such as running around corners, coming in through the wrong entrance or moving equipment in an incorrect manner. However, these rules form the basis for the safe running of a school and if they are to set the expected standard they must be accorded respect by adults and children. It would be an ideal state of affairs if we could ask children to conduct themselves sensibly and with consideration for others and add no further admonitions, but without the foundation of rules arising from the teacher's view of the best interests of all pupils, no child could be expected to behave in a way that did take everyone else into account.

We have no regulations about school uniform but the staff have debated at length the standards of dress we require from the children. Again the consequences of allowing children the freedom to make a personal choice are not always to our liking, because there are parents who will similarly exercise no control over the matter of dress and the choice is made without reference to any other criteria other than immediate personal preference. It is at this point that some teachers find it hard to swallow their prejudices about unsuitable clothing – and some we have not swallowed entirely, rationalizing our prohibitions by reference to impracticality. Hardly more than a handful of little girls appeared in beachwear on the warmest days of summer, anyone may wear trousers or jeans, shoes give no moments of horror, but plimsolls and wellingtons are perhaps as harmful and together with individuals and small groups we pursue through discussion the consequences of their decisions. In an affluent new town estate we expect to see the extremities of children's fashion, nurtured by the media, and we must, perforce, tolerate much of it. Most of the children in my group do not believe that a teacher has any right to regulate his mode of dress except where his performance in school would be affected by it and I cannot find in myself any authority for such regulation.

Transmission

The most important set of rules for us are those concerning the treatment of others. Transmission of the principles upon which considerate behaviour is based is achieved through example and exhortation but we also aim to give ample opportunities for making independent decisions involving these principles. If a child had to discover for himself what was acceptable behaviour in every situation, it would not only cause a great nuisance to others but would also divert him from other equally, if not more, valuable learning activities. Society is generally agreed about the basic principles of moral behaviour, that honesty, thought for others, regard for property, are virtues to be encouraged in children but we expect that a child will improve, modify and adapt the teachings of the older generation in the light of changing circumstances. At school assembly we often provide opportunities for children to rehearse their behaviour in situations which demand moral decisions, and because they are accustomed throughout their time with us to discussing and examining their actions without undue fear for the consequences, they have no reticence about such public experiments. They know that no suggestion is rejected out of hand if it is sincerely made (and very few are not). The whole age-range of the primary school is involved in this procedure and we have dealt with situations ranging from discovering a fire, delivering harvest parcels, asking parents to help at school functions, reconciling arguments, saying goodbye to a retiring caretaker, offering good wishes to a school journey party. In this way we lead children to say what ought to be done, and then they are given 'testing' times to see whether moral language is converted into moral behaviour, and how well established such behaviour is. This is the mainstay of our disciplinary structure, looking forward to ways in which children can show positive endorsement of their own principles, and it is, we believe, more effective than the coercion to which many of our children are accustomed at home. There are backsliders, children who forget or reject principles for expediency and in such cases we have to decide whether we can best support moral development by punishment, guidance, or removing the opportunity for further wrongdoing.

An important practical consequence of the school's philosophy is that children have many opportunities to abuse their positions of trust. Freedom of movement around a large building, including many areas where activities are not continuously supervised, freedom of access to equipment and materials, freedom to opt out or into many activities also implies the freedom to make mistakes, to pursue ideas or activities which are not acceptable to adults or other children and the freedom to waste opportunities. And all these things happen because we allow them to happen. It is a hard lesson for an experienced teacher to accept that these consequences are not evidence that the system does not work but that children are not mere receptacles for the well-intentioned moral values of their teachers. Therefore we have to structure the discipline of the school to cope with deviant behaviour.

Naturally what we would like to achieve is that the children temporarily in our care should become the kind of people who act with goodwill towards others, who can measure their own desires against the general good and proceed on the basis of such moral judgment rather than an acknowledgment of the possibility of being 'found out' and punished. I sometimes feel that it is ironical that in order to achieve this end I spend much effort in discovering bad behaviour and the perpetrators of it so that the issue may be analysed and motives uncovered before a child sinks into the position where he has become a persistent offender, who thinks of himself as such and has become impervious to the attitudes and judgments of others. An eleven-year-old girl once said to me 'If you don't get punished, you'll go on doing it' and the unstated inference was that if you are punished you cease to commit the crime. To some extent she is right because the administration of some restriction, or withdrawal of privileges is sufficient to remind the majority of children of the practical advisability of obedience if not the moral justification for such rules as there are. When a child takes the property of someone else I feel that the act has to be judged against the background of motive, circumstance, habitual behaviour as well as the hurt suffered by the other party. A purely objective judgment could be that the act is wrong, a right to property has been violated and that the wrongdoer deserves to be punished accordingly. There are implications behind each view that lead to complications – in the first case I have to be careful that a child must feel a sense of responsibility for his actions and that circumstance becomes increasingly less valid as an excuse for the wrongdoer, but the objective judge must ensure that a sledgehammer is not used to crack a nut, that the inevitability or severity of punishment does not bring about a cynical attitude towards rules and authority.

It is rare for staff, children and parents to agree about the role of punishment in a framework of discipline. For all of us it has a personal function as well as being a part of the enforcement of rules by authority. I have heard many expressions from parents indicating their desire to have their child's behaviour controlled, ranging from the unacceptable exhortations to hand out plentiful helpings of physical punishment to the equally unwelcome demand 'Just tell me if he won't behave and I'll sort him out'. The most satisfactory situation by far is the one where parents, after getting to know the staff concerned, can talk easily about what are usually common problems with a child. It helps to know how a child is disciplined at home even though we may not wish or be able to react similarly in school. Reasoned discussion has a place in some homes but by no means all and a child who is accustomed to swift retribution for his misdeeds finds it hard to talk about his behaviour honestly, to consider his motives and to allow other children to participate in this consideration.

Because we recognize our influence to be limited we try to enlist the cooperation of parents when faced with behaviour that is especially disturbing. This is not done merely in order to present the miscreant with a united adult front of anger or to increase the scope of punishment but for all parties to assess their response to this and similar situations so that a common solution may be found. Parents' reactions vary greatly from those who profess to have no knowledge of any misconduct by their child to those who would react harshly because of the involvement of the school. Recently we wrote to a number of parents explaining that their children were being severely punished because of the public nature of their offence, which had been a not untypical manifestation of group behaviour and the loss of individual responsibility. Damage, insults and public condemnation had ensued and we felt that the trust we had placed in them had been abused. Later I talked to children in my group, who had been involved, about the response of their parents to the letter. Some, I knew, had visited the school to ascertain the full extent of the problem, others had reinforced the punishment at home, several expressed verbally their support of our action, and some ignored the whole matter. If a child sees no similarity between home and school response to his behaviour he is placed in a dilemma; whether to reject the principles espoused by both parties and go his own way or whether to pursue those values with which he is more familiar. It is difficult to see how any punishment meted out by the school can in this case do more than encourage a resistance to authority.

Punishment

I suspect that much public concern over discipline in schools is actually concern about punishment, and the nature and severity of that punishment. My feeling is that for children below secondary school age, as far as the disciplinary structure and the enforcement of it through punishment are concerned, we must afford greater attention to the development of individual moral behaviour and rather less to 'showing the others' or upholding the dignity of the system and adults at all costs. The larger the institution the harder such an approach would be. We use no form of physical punishment and, although I have worked happily in establishments where this was not the case, I now feel that it would be both inappropriate and humiliating to do so. The mutual respect and liking between adults and children which is an important goal for us, could not be reached were we to respond with such an authoritarian response to behaviour which children are free, if not right, to commit.

We do restrict the free time of children who behave badly. This is a punishment that hurts, because it removes a child from his peer group and keeps him under adult surveillance. When I talk to my group about punishment they all agree that this is the most unpleasant punishment of all – and having seen far more severe forms in other schools I am tempted to believe that it is just a case of what you are used to. In using this restriction we sometimes pay lip-service to notions of appropriate, deserved, deterrent or reformative punishment but, to be honest, I think that it is little more than an extremely useful expedient.

To find an appropriate punishment for the act and for the individual would involve a vast waste of time. If a child takes someone's sweets and has no money of his own what appropriate punishment can there be? The act must not go unmarked, so give him a punishment that he has deserved, but discover that he never has sweets at home and so is not usually involved in 'shares' with other children. The degree of guilt is changing, but not the fact, so I look for a punishment that will deter him and others from repeating the act. To be effective I need to know just how strong the desire for sweets is before I can balance it with the severity of punishment (and is not the prospect of detection equally effective as a deterrent?). There is never enough time for such considerations but the one sure thing is that an adult must take note of the issue and respond to it in some way, through discussion, considering recompense or the short, sharp punishment that leaves the child feeling that the problem is over. Any hope of reformation can only be realized by an acknowledgment of the moral value violated and punishment alone rarely brings this about.

There are children who are led to see the desirability of conforming to the norm because the consequences of non-conformity are so unpleasant. I taught a boy who was so wayward, so lacking in control over his actions and emotions that it was decided to place him in a small unit for children with similar behavioural problems and the decision was justified to him on the grounds that there he would learn to cope with the social demands of a small group. He did so, in a remarkably short time, and returned to the class. Without much effort he adapted his skill to the more demanding classroom situation (only occasionally revealing his cynical view of the 'punishment' that he had undergone) and transferred to secondary school. His behaviour has reverted, is not unique there although greatly deplored, and there is no similar unit to which he can be transferred. He has learnt how to conform, can see the need for it to avoid banishment but regards himself as immune to regular punishment, which he has experienced to a considerable extent. I cannot think that any measures taken at school could have more than a short-term effect on his behaviour. I recount this story of failure because at the time he left us it looked to an outsider like success. He conformed in every way, he had learnt his lesson and my problem was solved. Learning to conform is no indication of internalized moral values!

Children develop a sense of 'fairness' early in life. Initially this may be no more than an awareness that there are greater and lesser portions of jelly and ice-cream but it is not long before the primary school child is demanding a degree of impartiality in the treatment he and his peers receive from a teacher, voiced in the irritating but frequently repeated phrase 'She did it as well'. The hope is that the wider the blame can be spread the more diluted the retribution will be and I have come to accept that this response is not tale-telling in the usual sense, although it may arise from a rather less than high-minded desire to ensure that I am in full possession of all the relevant facts before I proceed to judgment. If I attempt to sort out an argument between children which has disturbed the general peace I find that it is much harder to prompt an honest response to the question 'But what did *you* do?' In these circumstances the emphasis again is on the actions of the other party and if I accepted the first version I would find that I had a totally blameless, saint-like character and a wholly villainous adversary to deal with. No doubt the traditional figure of authority, remote and all-powerful, in the schoolday memories of the parents of our children would not have been trifled with in this manner but I suspect that as many lies were told out of fear then, and remained undiscovered because of the remoteness of authority. It may be time-consuming to encourage the truth, prompting, reminding and simply waiting, but at least in that way we come to know the children and they move nearer to knowing, and accepting themselves.

Conclusion

I cannot overstress the role of language in our disciplinary structure. Without talking about shared or individual experience the children cannot relate to each other, recognize reactions in others, or learn to exercise control over their actions; thus talking is the essence of nursery education. We build on it in the primary school by evaluating, imagining the feelings of others, looking at long-term and short-term effects of behaviour and searching for alternatives. It is our misfortune to be required to justify this approach against charges of being 'soft'. We use methods of teaching that work and we believe are right for our children; we transmit values that society supports through means that are compatible with our teaching methods but we cannot achieve the desired results with every child. There have always been offenders and in a free state there always will be – they are no new product of the progressive primary school and although it might be thought that the worst offenders 'deserve' severe, maybe corporal, punishment this has not solved the problem in the past. No doubt it will take a long period of concerted effort from home and school and all the social agencies before any change is seen.

Our approach is successful for most of the children, most of the time. Visitors remark on their courtesy, their helpfulness towards younger children, their ability to use initiative in demanding situations and their eagerness to share. Those are some of our goals and so we are reassured and gratified, but not satisfied. We do not have many hard disciplinary problems. It is usual only for the class teacher to see the little failures, the untruths, unkind behaviour and deviousness that only angels are without but it is our difficult, never-ending task to see that such behaviour does not become the accepted norm. In the caring school every teacher will be involved in this task, working in her own way, achieving the desired results, slowly and all too often without the support of those most influential agents, the parents.

Notes on Contributors

JOHN ANDERSON is principal of the College of St Mark and St John, a college of education of 600 men and women students on degree courses. The college was in Chelsea until five years ago, when it moved to Plymouth. John Anderson has been its principal for six years. Before that he was Research Fellow at the School of Cultural and Community Studies at Sussex University, and before that was a lecturer at University College, Nairobi. He is a consultant for UNESCO and the ILEO. He has published a book *The Struggle For The Schools* (Longman 1970) and has contributed chapters to a number of books on education.

BERNARD BAXTER is headmaster of Gosforth High School, Newcastle-upon-Tyne, a comprehensive school of 1,300 boys and girls aged thirteen to eighteen in a city suburb. He has been at Gosforth for four years. For five years previously he was headmaster of Longbenton High School, a comprehensive of 1,100 boys and girls which he opened, on a large municipal housing estate bordering Newcastle. Before that he taught at Gateway School, Leicester and Shirebrook School, Derbyshire. He is a Justice of the Peace.

JOAN DEAN is the Chief Inspector of the Surrey Local Education Authority, which comprises 500 different educational institutions and is the sixth largest authority in the country. She is one of only three women Chief Inspectors in the country and has thirty-three inspectors in her team. She has held this post for seven years and before that was Senior Primary Adviser to Berkshire. She was President of the National Association of Inspectors and Educational Advisers in 1971/2. She is a member of the Soulbury Committee and Chairman of the BBC Schools Broadcasting Council Programme Committee I. She has published sixteen books and many articles and frequently appears on radio and television. Her husband, an engineer, is manager of a computer firm.

TOM GANNON has been headmaster of Milefield Middle School, Grimethorpe, Barnsley, since 1968, the first 'purpose-built' middle school in the country, which has 450 boys and girls aged eleven to thirteen. It is situated in a mixed rural, industrial and mining area, typical of South Yorkshire. Before this he was for twelve years headmaster of Hemsworth (Sacred Heart), an all-age school of 240 boys and girls aged five to fifteen. Tom Gannon has published a number of books and articles on schools, and is Chairman of the BBC Schools Broadcasting Council Programme Committee II. He was awarded the OBE in 1974.

GEOFFREY GOODALL is principal of Lord Williams's School, Thame, Oxfordshire, a comprehensive school of 2,100 boys and girls aged eleven to eighteen in a 'small and peaceful country town'. He was appointed headmaster of the school in 1963, when it was a selective grammar school of 213 boys; it was reorganized to form the present comprehensive school in 1971. Before that he taught at Haberdashers' Askes, Hatcham and at Uppingham. He is Chairman of the Legal and Parliamentary Committee of the Secondary Heads Association, a delegate of the Oxford University Local Delegacy for Examinations and represents the GCE Boards on the Convocation of the Schools Council. He is a member of the Keohane Committee on 17 + examinations.

MOLLY HATTERSLEY is headmistress of Creighton School at Muswell Hill, Haringey, London, a school of 1,450 boys and girls aged eleven to eighteen in what she describes as 'a very mixed area', where there is free parental choice. In 1976, a book about the school, *The Creighton Report*, by Hunter Davies was published. Molly Hattersley has been headmistress of Creighton since 1974; before that she was senior mistress of Myers Grove School, Sheffield, for five years deputy headmistress of Kidbrooke School, and then for six years headmistress of Hurlingham School, a comprehensive school of 1,000 girls in Fulham under the ILEA. She is Chairman of the Professional Committee of the Secondary Heads Association and was Chairman of the Committee of the Association of Headmistresses. She is the wife of Roy Hattersley, the present Secretary of State for Prices and Consumer Protection.

ARNOLD JENNINGS is headmaster of Ecclesfield School, Sheffield, a comprehensive school of 1,900 boys and girls aged eleven to eighteen situated on the north side of Sheffield which serves an area mostly suburban, part industrial, part rural, which gives it a balanced cross-section of the population both academically and socially. Arnold Jennings was appointed headmaster of Ecclesfield Grammar School in 1959, a selective grammar school of 950 boys and girls under the West Riding education authority; it was reorganized in 1967 to form the present comprehensive school, which at its largest had 2,200 pupils. Before that Arnold Jennings taught at Chesterfield Grammar School and was headmaster of Tapton House School, Chesterfield, a grammar school of 450 boys and girls. Arnold Jennings is Hon. Secretary of the Secondary Heads Association and was President of the Headmasters Association in 1977. He was on the Executive of the National Union of Teachers for many years and has belonged to its Grammar Schools Committee and Secondary Advisory Committee for thirty years. He is Chairman of the Examinations Committee of the Schools Council, on which he has served since its formation in 1964. He was a member of the Waddell Committee on 16 + examinations. He was for several years a member of Sheffield Education Committee. He was awarded the CBE in 1977.

PETER KENNEDY is headmaster of Great Wakering Primary School, Essex, a school of 500 boys and girls aged five to eleven in an area which was recently a village and has now become part of a commuter area. Peter Kennedy has been headmaster of Great Wakering since 1966; before that he was head of a small primary school in Holland, Lincs. He has been a member of the Executive of the National Union of Teachers for seven years and will be President of the National Union of Teachers next year.

SISTER MARIE PHILIPPA (Marie Philippa Waters) became headmistress of Notre Dame High School, Sheffield, in September 1978. This is a former direct grant Roman Catholic girls grammar school which is now being reorganized as an aided school to form a coeducational comprehensive school of 820 boys and girls. From 1972 to 1978 Sister Marie was headmistress of St Gregory's Roman Catholic School, Kirkby, Liverpool, a comprehensive school of 1,700 girls aged eleven to eighteen serving a large municipal housing estate occupied by families from the centre of Liverpool who had been rehoused. Before that she was headmistress of Notre Dame Collegiate School, Everton Valley, Liverpool, a direct grant Roman Catholic girls grammar school. Sister Marie belongs to the Congregation of the Sisters of Notre Dame. She is a member of the Council of the Secondary Heads Association.

TOM ROLF is a Senior Adviser for Secondary Education to the Devon Education Authority. He has held the post since 1976; he was for eleven years before that headmaster of Colne Valley High School, at which he had earlier been head of mathematics, a comprehensive school of 1,800 boys and girls aged eleven to eighteen on the western outskirts of Huddersfield. Before that for four years he was deputy headmaster at Holloway School, London, an Islington comprehensive of 1,200 boys.

ELIZABETH WALLIS is the Hon. Press Officer for the Confederation for the Advancement of State Education, on whose Executive she serves. She lives in Richmond, Surrey, and has two sons, now seventeen and fifteen, attending secondary schools. She is a professional librarian and was Deputy Film Librarian of the BBC. She is now a freelance professional indexer. Her husband is a writer on the built environment.

ANNE WEBB is deputy headmistress of Fields End Junior Mixed and Infants School, Hemel Hempstead, Herts., a school of 180 boys and girls aged three to eleven on the edge of a new town. She has been there for three years and before that taught at London Colney Junior Mixed and Infants' School and before that at Pontefract in her native West Riding. She was President of the Students' Union at Goldsmiths' College. She has taken part in visitations to institutes of higher education by the Council for National Academic Awards as a representative of the National Union of Teachers. She has written articles in various educational publications.

Index

pupils—cont.
external pressures 54, 77–81
fear of bullying 88
less able 20, 29, 83–4, 93
matching curriculum to 45–7, 65,
90, 93–4
middle school 37–8
motivation 5, 9, 31, 45, 61, 96
participation 7
peer group pressures 25, 30, 38,
50, 61, 108
perceptions 36, 37
progress discussions 16
pupil-teacher relationships 7–8,
11, 48–9, 53, 57, 62, 77, 95
rights 11, 102–3, 106
and rule-making 49, 64–5
self-awareness 6, 46, 93
self-image 50
starting school 30
welfare 1, 5, 8, 36
see also difficult children; pastoral
care

referral systems 17–18, 51, 55–6, 69,
96, 97–8
relationships
generally 46, 49–50, 108
home-school 8–9, 37, 58, 64, 77,
102–3, 105–6
pupil-teacher 7–8, 11, 48–9, 53,
57, 62, 77, 95
responsibility, for discipline 17, 49,
71
rights, individual 7, 11, 102–3, 106
rules 17, 28, 45, 49, 63, 71–2, 108–9
pupil involvement 49, 64–5

sanctions *see* punishment
school leaving age, raising of 20,
23
schools
academic structure 16, 20, 93–4
aims 5, 24, 29, 46, 53, 55, 71, 92–3,
107
as caring institutions 107
and changing society 11–12, 15,
25, 52–3, 77–81, 93, 95
checks on 70
and community 8–9, 37, 65–6, 85,
90, 106, 107

comprehensive 6–7, 28, 36, 44,
53–4, 58–9, 83, 85–6
and deprivation 6–7
environment, effect of 49, 54–5,
66, 94–5
framework of values 27–9, 49–50,
53, 55, 58, 89–90, 92–3, 106,
107–8, 109–12
functions 5, 7, 46, 53
home-school relationships 8–9, 37,
58, 64, 77, 102–3, 105–6
interactive role 8–9, 15, 20–1
middle 35, 37–8
primary 71–3, 107
and 'real world' 27, 98, 103
selective 54
social climate within 35–9, 106–7
special 68, 75–6
variations among 60, 62–3, 67, 89
selective schools 54
self-discipline 25, 30–2, 39–40, 47,
58, 72, 90, 99, 106
social climate, of schools 35–9, 106–7
measurement 36
social workers *see* welfare services
society
casualties of 23, 58, 105
change in 2–3, 9, 11–12, 14–15,
24–5, 52–3, 77–81, 93, 95
norms 5, 25–6
special education 68–9, 75–7, 80
staff meetings 16, 64, 71
standards
alleged lowering 2, 14, 36, 53, 82
1960s 84
teachers' competence 105
Sutton, Dr 86

Taylor Committee 11
teacher-training 9–11
in-service 11, 105
Nottingham University Teacher
Education Project 86
problems of 9–10
selection for 11, 19, 86
teachers
checks on 69–70, 103
competence 105
control techniques 5–6, 7–8, 17,
26, 30, 32–3, 39–41, 48, 72–3,
86–9

Index by Ann Edwards